THE UNLEASHED ENTREPRENEUR

THE UNLEASHED
ENTREPRENEUR

WosterMedia LLC
Tampa, Florida
woostermediabooks.com

ISBN: 979-8-9929737-1-6

Published by WoosterMedia LLC
woostermediabooks.com

WoosterMedia

TABLE OF CONTENTS

INTRODUCTION

If you've picked up this book, it's because something deep inside you is stirring.

Maybe you feel the pull to create something of your own. Perhaps you're standing at a crossroads, wondering if it's time to leave the safety of the familiar and step into something new. Or maybe you've already started your entrepreneurial journey, but the road has been more challenging than you expected.

Wherever you are on this path, know this: You are not alone.

The Unleashed Entrepreneur is a collection of stories, lessons, and insights from those who have dared to take the leap—people who, just like you, had a vision for something greater. Some started their businesses from a place of passion, others from necessity, and many because they simply couldn't ignore the call to do more with their lives. What they all have in common is the courage to take the first step.

Entrepreneurship: The Ultimate Transformation

Entrepreneurship is not just about building a business. It's about becoming the person who can develop and sustain that business. It's about resilience, reinvention, and stepping into your true potential.

Both of us have lived through our own transformations. We have each left behind careers that no longer served us, embraced uncertainty, and built businesses that provide financial freedom and align with our greater purpose.

Wendi left a twenty-five-year career in the pharmaceutical industry, walking away from a stable six-figure job, company perks, and a predictable future to step into a world where she could create her own impact. Patricia transitioned from corporate sales to publishing, turning her love for storytelling into a career that has helped countless authors bring their messages to the world.

Neither of us had a perfect roadmap. There was no guarantee that things would work out. But we leaped anyway because the alternative—staying in a life that no longer fit us—was simply not an option.

What You'll Find in This Book

This book isn't just about entrepreneurship in the traditional sense. It's about building a life on your terms. It's about identifying what truly matters to you and using your unique gifts to create something that serves others while fulfilling you.

Inside these pages, you'll find:

- Real stories from entrepreneurs who have faced fears, overcome obstacles, and built businesses that align with their values.

- Lessons from failure and success, because both are equally valuable on this journey.
- Tangible strategies and insights to help you navigate your own path—whether you're just starting or looking to grow.
- Encouragement and inspiration for the days when doubt creeps in (because it will).

We didn't write this book to give you a cookie-cutter business blueprint. Instead, we want to equip you with the mindset, tools, and confidence to carve out your path—one that feels aligned, impactful, and deeply fulfilling.

The Truth About This Journey

We won't sugarcoat it: Entrepreneurship is hard.

There will be days when you feel like giving up. Moments when you question if you're cut out for this. Times when the people around you won't understand your vision.

But here's what we also know:

1. Your greatest opportunities often come disguised as challenges. The moments that feel like setbacks are actually setting you up for something greater.
2. You don't have to do this alone. Surrounding yourself with the right people—mentors, peers, and a community that supports you—can make all the difference.

3. The best investment you can make is in yourself. The more you grow, the more your business will grow. Never stop learning, evolving, and stepping into the next level of who you are meant to be.

If you take only one thing from this book, let it be this: *You are capable of more than you realize. The life and business you dream about are possible but won't happen by accident. You have to choose them. You have to take action. And you have to believe that you are worthy of the success waiting for you.*

Your Next Step Starts Now

This book is not meant to sit on a shelf. It's intended to be a guide, a source of inspiration, and a tool to help you move forward.

As you read these stories, let them prove that if others can do it, so can you. Take notes, reflect on what resonates with you, and, most importantly, take action. Even the smallest step forward is still a step.

We are honored to share this journey with you. We hope that by finishing this book, you'll feel more confident, empowered, and ready to take your next bold step.

The world needs what only *you* can create.

To your success and impact,

Wendi Blum Weiss & Patricia Wooster

TIME WAS THE ULTIMATE MOTIVATOR FOR ME—OR THE SHORTNESS OF IT AND HOW QUICKLY IT GOES BY.

Wendi Blum Weiss

CHAPTER 1

IF TODAY WERE MY LAST DAY
BY WENDI BLUM WEISS

If today were my last day, I would resign.
So I did.

It was twenty-five years in the making. My two-plus decades in the pharmaceutical industry had been good to me. The job had given me stability as a single mom—a dependable six-figure income, a company car, travel, an expense account, and other perks.

I was successful on paper, but I couldn't shake the feeling that something was missing.

I had dress-rehearsed my resignation day many times. Here I was in San Francisco at a medical conference. It was Friday afternoon, the last day, and the energy in the room had shifted to rushed goodbyes. I waited until the very last moment, just a few minutes before I needed to jump into a taxi to head to the airport. Then I asked my boss, Jeff, "Do you have a few minutes to talk?"

As Jeff's eyes met mine, it was clear he sensed something big was coming. At that moment, I knew there was no turning back.

I shared with Jeff that I had written a book about reinventing your life and felt compelled to change careers so I could write books, be a motivational speaker, and offer some sort of success or sales coaching. For more than a year, I had been thinking about leaving. I greatly respected the people and the company, but I was living in two worlds at the same time—my corporate career and the brand-new entrepreneurial path that was calling me forward.

Speaking the words out loud made it real. With immense gratitude for my long-standing career and company, I resigned.

One Year Earlier

One year before my resignation, I walked into my first entrepreneurial conference, called "Be the Change You Want to See in the World," with no idea my life was about to change.

The room was packed, with 300 well-dressed men and women from all walks of life. Everyone seemed excited to be there. Then, suddenly, silence fell as the lights dimmed. All eyes turned toward the big screen at the front of the room, where the band Nickelback's music video "If Today Was Your Last Day" began to play.

The music filled the space, and one single salty tear rolled down my cheek. It felt like the message in the lyrics was speaking directly to me. Little did I know that what I heard that day would become the theme of my life.

As I listened, chills ran down my spine. It was as if the song was awakening my life's purpose. My soul was reignited as if I were twenty-one again.

Truth be told, I hadn't even noticed how numb I'd been for so many years, how I spent my time just going through the motions. That day, something deep inside of me came alive. It was like I'd discovered a whole new world.

When I graduated college, I had a laundry list of basic goals:

- Land a job at a Fortune 500 company.
- Get a good salary and job security.
- Climb the corporate ladder.
- Have medical insurance.

My personal life had a checklist too:
- Get married.
- Have kids.
- Buy a house.
- Build a stable career.

These were the things I thought would lead to happiness. But life has a way of throwing curveballs—a divorce here, mounting pressures there.

None of us know how much time we really have. It's a lesson I learned early on in my life. Just one month before I was born, my six-year-old brother died in a drowning accident. In my twenties, I lost my father to cancer. I remember making a vow as a teenager: I would never take life for granted.

Now, suddenly, my life was taking a new turn. I was intrigued—and invigorated!

Becoming an Entrepreneur

For years, I defined myself by my corporate career. Stability, achievements, and a structured path were all I knew. I had never paid much attention to entrepreneurship before. It was appealing, but these were uncharted waters—I had no idea what it entailed. I knew one thing for sure: I would be asked to leave the comfort of familiarity and step into a completely different version of myself.

I wrote out my mission statement and started to spread the world. I figured since I had already written a book, I would next start speaking about my transition and host my first conference. It seemed like a natural first step as I was used to putting together meetings and entertaining doctors. I could figure it out.

I remember every detail vividly now in my new role as a Success and Strategy Coach. I rented out a big banquet space at the Marriott Hutchinson Island and brought in five top-notch speakers. I had no idea how to sell tickets for the event. When I produced events for my former company (BMS), I had an unlimited budget, and now I just had my own checkbook with limited funds.

I hustled hard to get people to the three-day event I called a "Health, Wellness & Business Conference." I was exhausted. I spoke a dozen or more times for groups like the Chamber of Commerce and women's organizations, and guest-appeared on multiple online forums to fill the space for my conference, which I did. I wanted a "wow experience" for my first event, so I went over my budget but was hoping it would pay off.

Yes, I lost money on the event, but more importantly, I got great reviews and built a strong reputation. I also lost my voice at the end of day one and just about collapsed from exhaustion. Entrepreneurship taught me a valuable lesson that weekend. It was a crash course on organizing events in this new, unfamiliar terrain.

It was hard, very hard, but so was corporate. Yet this *hard* was very different. I was operating from a higher place, my calling versus a paycheck—living my "If today were my last day" Nickelback philosophy.

In the long run, even with exhaustion and overspending, I would do it the same way again and consider it worth it.

Flash-Forward to 2024

I now have fifteen years of entrepreneurship under my belt. It's been a journey of experimenting, failing fast, and moving forward, all leading me to where I am today: doing what I love, with talented, smart people I love. I have the great honor of helping authors write best-selling books, speaking on stages, building communities, and impacting lives.

Sometimes God has a better plan than we can even imagine for ourselves. My journey evolved in ways I couldn't have predicted. But one thing I knew for sure:

I was fifty years old when I resigned, and here I am at sixty-four, writing this chapter in our fifth co-author book in three years.

Everything touches everything.

I took my years of sales and marketing working for big pharma and applied them to entrepreneurship. With every cell in my body, I now know this was the divinely orchestrated plan, the path I needed to take in order to find my calling and my divine purpose. If today were my last day, I would still be doing *this*.

You don't know what you don't know—until you do.

Years ago I did not know this world even existed. Now I do.

Books as a Catalyst

Books have radically changed my life. Back in my corporate days, I didn't read much—not because I didn't love books, but because work demanded so much of my time and energy. Between medical journals and research papers, I rarely had the mental space to pick up a book for myself.

Stepping into entrepreneurship changed that. I started diving into reading again—sometimes a new book every week—especially books about mindset, business building, and stories of successful people. I had several favorites I would read over and over again. Holding a book began to feel deeply personal, like having a one-on-one conversation with someone who had been where I wanted to go.

I also started giving my favorite books as gifts. On my oldest son Daniel's twenty-first birthday, we met for dinner at Houston's in North Miami. As he sat down, I handed him a gigantic gift bag filled with twenty-one books—all of them my favorites, including *The Power of Your Subconscious Mind* by Joseph Murphy and *Think and Grow Rich* by Napoleon Hill, except for the very last one. That one was a handwritten book I had written for him called *21 Wishes for Your 21st Birthday*.

His eyes widened. "Mom, you wrote this book for me? Wow, thank you."

Books change lives. Mine and others. They hold knowledge, love, and legacy within their pages.

Today, I'm obsessed with books—reading them, writing them, and helping others bring their own stories to life. Whether it's a solo book or a chapter in a co-author project, I've seen the magic that happens when someone pours their heart into words. Books are transformative, not just for the reader but for the author too.

The Power of Community, Connection, and Collaboration

After leaving corporate and stepping into entrepreneurship, I knew one thing for sure: I didn't want to go at it alone. I wanted to build a community and forge collaborative partnerships that would make the journey easier and more meaningful.

After writing five books on my own, I realized I wanted my next project to be a co-author book. I had been drawn to the co-author book model for some time and decided it was the right fit for my vision. I knew what I wanted in a business partner—someone who shared my values, understood the process, and could help create something impactful. For five years, I actively searched until I met Patricia Wooster online during the Covid shutdown.

Within two years of working together, we completed three co-author book projects. The success of these collaborations inspired us to fully merge our businesses and form a new company: Mindset to Millions.

The reason co-author books are so appealing—when done the right way—lies in the power of community. Consider this: 90 percent of people dream about writing a book, but less than 2 percent actually do it. Why? Because the process is overwhelming. Writing is only a fraction of the work. Afterward, there's editing, formatting, graphic design, marketing, securing placement in bookstores, organizing events, and hosting book signings. It's a daunting task, especially for someone doing it alone.

But when you have both a guide to navigate the writing and publishing process and a community to support you along the way, it transforms the entire experience. Suddenly, it's not only doable—it's enjoyable.

Patricia is a true wizard when it comes to writing and publishing books. Her superpower is simplifying the complex world of publishing, turning ideas into polished manuscripts. My superpower is building community and organizing events—bringing people together to collaborate, connect, and create. Together, we've blended our strengths to amplify impact.

That is the beauty of partnerships.

Why Write a Book?

1. You have a story to share.
2. You have valuable expertise.
3. You can inspire others.
4. It's a powerful sales tool.
5. You want to leave a legacy.

Being part of a co-author book or writing your own book is also the secret sauce to growing your business. It's a fast and effective way to establish authority, build rapport, and share your story in an authentic way—without being salesy. Books are the ultimate tool for getting booked on stages, featured on podcasts, and attracting more visibility to your business. They're the best form of advertising and can also be given as meaningful, valuable gifts to prospective clients.

Patricia and I have helped countless people step into their new identity as best-selling authors and professional speakers, showcasing their expertise and elevating their voices as thought leaders. Her talent for bringing stories to life has been an incredible asset to our work. Working as a team, we've seen how the right book can open doors to new opportunities, build confidence, and create lasting change.

Books are more than words on a page—they're tools for transformation. They create emotional connections with readers, build trust, and leave lasting impressions. Writing a book changes how the world sees you but also how you see yourself.

Writing a book is timeless, and your voice is limitless. Together, you can change the world.

Creating Platforms for Others

Beyond books, we help people find their voices on stage—a challenge for many. In fact, studies show that the fear of public speaking (glossophobia) is often ranked as the number one phobia, surpassing even the fear of death.

I remember being terrified when I first stepped onto a stage. Yet, speaking is one of the most powerful ways to share a message and make an impact. That's why we've expanded our writing programs to include opportunities to speak at our signature events—whether it's delivering a keynote, joining a panel discussion, or leading a breakout session.

There's nothing more rewarding than watching someone step into their power, own their moment, and light up a room.

Time and a Sense of Urgency

Before the *Be the Change* event, I had never thought about sharing my story or speaking on stage. As I watched, listened, and learned, it was as if time suddenly seemed more critical.

The speaker shared her story and why she was so passionate about helping people "become the change" they wanted to see in the world. It clicked. I was sitting in my seat, asking myself, *Is it too late for me? Am I too old?*

I looked around the room and observed every age bracket—from people in their twenties to their seventies—attentively listening. I heard a soft voice whisper, "It's never too late." I had been too busy being busy to slow down long enough to hear that small, still voice of wisdom speak until now.

Looking at the Statistics

Let's look at the reality of time:

- The average lifespan of a woman in the U.S. is 80.2 years.
  » That's 962.4 months or 4,181.86 weeks.
- The average lifespan of a man in the U.S. is 77.43 years.
  » That's 929.16 months or 4,037.4 weeks.

If you're fifty, like I was when I resigned, you statistically have about 30 years remaining. And certainly, all of us want to make those happy years.

So let me ask you: On a scale from one to ten, how happy and fulfilled are you at work? Because right now, most of us are exchanging our most valuable asset, *time*, for money.

Close your eyes for a moment. Think about that.

Trading Time for Money

Are you truly in alignment? Are you living your life to the fullest?

- Have you done the things that are truly in your heart?
- Where are you giving your time away?
- Where are you saying yes when you should be saying no?
- What big dreams, goals, and desires have you been brushing under the rug?

I know what it's like to sleepwalk through life, just going through the motions. But here's the reality: It's never too late to step fully into your purpose.

Maybe for you, that means writing a book. Maybe it's speaking on stages. Maybe it's changing careers, launching a new business, or simply living life on your terms.

Whatever it is, I challenge you to ask yourself: If today were your last day, what would you wish you had accomplished? Because the clock is ticking.

The Gift of Time

But let's flip the script.

What if today *wasn't* your last day? What if, instead, you were just gifted another decade of life?

Here's what that looks like in numbers:

- 1 decade = **10 years**
- 10 years = **520 weeks**
- 520 weeks = **3,650 days**
- 3,650 days = **87,600 hours**

Take a moment. Grab a pen and paper.

Write down **ten things you would prioritize** if you were blessed with **an additional 87,600 hours**.

I've worked with people at every stage of life—twenties, thirties, forties, fifties, sixties, seventies, even eighties—and if there's one thing I've learned, it's this: **It's never too late.**

Living My Legacy

If today were my last day, I would want my stories to leave an imprint of inspiration and impact.

What I do today isn't just a career—it's my calling, my legacy. I wake up each morning knowing that my work helps others step into their power, share their message, and create a ripple effect of change. Every story, every stage, and every book holds the potential to transform lives far beyond what we can see.

I often think back to that song, "If Today Was Your Last Day." It still guides my decisions and reminds me of the urgency of purpose.

If today were my last day, I'd know I lived fully and meaningfully, inspiring men and women to share their voices, tell their stories, and leave a legacy of their own.

What is the "why" behind what you do?

Entrepreneurship can feel lonely, but it doesn't have to be.

One of the things I'm most proud of is the community we've built. I believe that bringing people together—whether authors, speakers, or thought leaders—creates a space where magic happens. Connections are formed, support systems are built, and ideas are amplified.

Starting from scratch was hard. I wish I would have had a community just like ours.

Through our academy, masterminds, retreats, and book group coaching, we've created spaces where authors, speakers, and thought leaders come together to learn, grow, and support one another. Our community is about more than business—it's about connection, shared purpose, and making a difference.

What unique framework or service do you offer to your community or clients?

We are the only comprehensive program that offers a variety of book-writing programs that include events, speaking gigs, podcast guesting, customized book signings, and an entire community.

What is the best professional tip or advice you have received?

Hire a coach or consultant to show you the shortcuts.

Time was the ultimate motivator for me—or the shortness of it and how quickly it goes by. I didn't learn about entrepreneurship until later in life and wanted to buy back as much time as possible.

I had just turned fifty and asked myself, *How can I consolidate ten years of learning how to monetize my own coaching into just one?*

I applied three principles to "hack back" my time:

1. **Invest in a coach**: I knew I couldn't do it on my own, so I hired an expert to show me the quickest way to stand out and grow my authority.
2. **Go from one-to-one to one-to-many**: I wrote a book, started speaking on stages, built a community (and an email list), and created a group coaching program.
3. **Start before you're ready**: Even though it was scary, I went all in and followed Nike's adage to "Just Do It."

Knowing that time was crucial, I made the difficult decision to invest $37,000 in coaching the first year (2010) in order to shortcut the system. It was the scariest and hardest decision I ever made. However, it was the springboard to a six-figure business and the start of my new entrepreneurial career.

My Message for You

Whatever your age, personal life circumstances, or story, I see you, I feel you, and I believe in you.

And remember: You're never too young, you're never too old, and **it's never too late**.

Where can people connect with you?

I can be found at WendiBlum.com
and LinkedIn @WendiBlum.

YOU DON'T HAVE TO HAVE IT ALL FIGURED OUT TO TAKE THE NEXT STEP. ALL YOU NEED IS A WILLINGNESS TO SHOW UP, TAKE IMPERFECT ACTION, AND TRUST THE PROCESS.

CHAPTER 2

UNLEASHING IMPACT – A JOURNEY TO PURPOSEFUL TRANSFORMATION BY PATRICIA WOOSTER

In March of last year, I stood at a crossroads. I had just exited a SaaS company I co-founded, a venture that represented years of hard work and growth but no longer aligned with my deepest passions. With my sons almost grown, I was uniquely positioned to go all in on creating a lifestyle by design—one that represented me, my family, and who I most wanted to serve.

This wasn't my first reinvention. In my twenties, I worked in enterprise software sales for big companies. My thirties were a series of side hustles that generated extra income while I was raising my boys. By my forties, I was a best-selling author with Simon & Schuster and a coach helping executives and athletes write their books. Each decade brought a new season of growth, but this past year was different. For the first time, I had clarity on my calling: to empower others to take their expertise and transform it into something meaningful, whether through books, speeches, or scalable programs.

Every experience prior had prepared me for this moment. Over the years (without realizing it), I quietly built my authority as someone who could help others create an impact with their genius. While writing books for myself, I was learning how to teach others. As I taught myself how to create college-accredited courses, cohorts, and certification programs, I was adding those skill sets to my arsenal. My SaaS company taught me business strategy, high-level content creation, and marketing and messaging. Bit by bit, I was building this new business, but I didn't know it.

Partnering with Purpose

And that is where my partnership with Wendi Blum Weiss came into the picture, ushering in a year of transformation, growth, and collaboration. While I was whiling away and developing my craft, she was also focused on development. After twenty-five years in pharma, she sought every opportunity to learn and grow as an incredible speaker, entrepreneur, and coach. Between the two of us, we represented over five decades of experience in entrepreneurship, over twenty published books, and hundreds of client success stories.

Wendi brings her unique superpower to our partnership: an unparalleled ability to inspire and energize people. She is a master speaker who has taken stages globally, and her experience perfectly complements my focus on books and brand strategy. Together, we developed programs like Unleash Expert Academy and co-authored book projects that equip our clients to stand out in crowded markets while co-creating in community.

Wendi and I are kindred spirits, deeply committed to helping people harness their earned expertise. We share a vision of empowering entrepreneurs, authors, and thought leaders to elevate their brands and create lasting impact. We've launched programs, coached clients, and published books—all with the aim of helping others stand out as trusted authorities in their fields. It's about creating a ripple effect of transformation by shining the light on incredible people doing amazing things.

Our work is rooted in three principles: clarity, collaboration, and community. First, we help our clients clarify their messaging and offers. Attracting the right audience is nearly impossible without a clear, concise message. Second, we build their confidence by providing the tools and support they need to step into the spotlight and connect as experts. And finally, we foster a sense of community, because entrepreneurship can be lonely, and success is never a solo endeavor.

Understanding leverage is one of the pivotal moments that led us to stand out in our industry. A book, for example, is never just a book—it's an opportunity generator. It can lead to speaking engagements, bulk sales, programs, coaching clients, and so much more. As Wendi and I refined our methodology, we built systems that helped our clients write books and taught them how to turn those books into tools that built their authority and businesses. This mindset shift became a cornerstone of our work and is why our clients are opening doors to large opportunities.

Lessons Learned

Most of my career can be categorized as a "lesson learned." I spent my first six years as an entrepreneur as an "investor." Meaning, I invested my money and time into other people's programs but did nothing for myself in return. One of the hardest lessons I learned was that perfectionism is the enemy of progress. I've seen too many people wait to feel "ready" before taking the next step—whether it's writing their book, launching a course, or stepping onto a stage. But the truth is, you're never truly ready. Success comes from showing up, taking imperfect action, and learning as you go.

As a recovering perfectionist, I have found a few things that help:

Let people know what you are working on and let them know early. Sharing at the ideation stage is key because you are still open to feedback. Most perfectionists wait until the project is complete and they are no longer willing to make changes. This destroys innovation or wastes a lot of time in making changes to something that appears to be done. The better I get at pulling things together quickly, asking for input, and then testing with our audience, the faster we can scale and grow our business. I'm still working on it but feel confident I'll get there.

Another key lesson was the importance of niching down. I wanted to serve everyone early in my career, but I quickly realized the value of focusing on a specific audience. Today, I work primarily with entrepreneurs and thought leaders ready to make an impact at scale. By zeroing in on this niche, we've been able to create customized solutions that drive real results.

And the most important lesson is to listen to your intuition. If something sounds too good to be true, it most likely is. This is where you can lean on your community and get a second and third opinion. Big decisions like taking on new business partners, investing in project buildouts, and signing contracts can have lasting implications. I have made mistakes in all these areas, which takes a toll on your emotions, resources, and bank account. Those red flags pop up for a reason, so take a pause and think before acting.

The Destination (So Far)

As I write this, I am fifty-two years old and feel more energized and aligned than ever. My youngest son graduates high school this year, so we are almost empty nesters. The gift of being an entrepreneur is being location-independent and able to work when and how you want.

I look forward to designing this next stage of our lives as my husband and I work to integrate our work and free time. I used to think that people in their fifties were so old and winding down toward retirement. Now

I find myself making long-term professional plans and taking steps for more development and growth. The journey isn't over. In fact, I feel like it's just beginning.

And as an example to my boys, I want them to see parents who are thriving and not afraid to pursue their dreams. The path is often winding (and often doesn't make sense), but it's all in search of finding where you belong. It's trusting the process and understanding that eventually things work out exactly as intended.

If there's one thing I've learned in the past year, it's this: You don't have to have it all figured out to take the next step. All you need is a willingness to show up, take imperfect action, and trust the process.

Because when you do, you unleash your expertise as well as your greatness—and that's where the magic happens.

What is the "why" behind what you do?

I used to say it was to create impact, but for me it goes deeper than that. I want to know that my life matters— not only professionally but to the people around me in my personal life. We lost my ninety-seven-year-old grandmother this year, the family matriarch by every definition of the word. She represented a well-lived life. It wasn't about standing out in one key area but adding value to all areas of life.

Here are the questions I am using as my North Star to keep me focused on my "why."

- Family: How am I showing up daily for my husband and sons? Am I having meaningful conversations and taking an active interest in their lives? It's too easy to fall into patterns of exchanging itineraries and not having thoughtful connections due to busy schedules. I'm trying to slow down and enjoy the moments every day.
- Relationships: Who do I need to connect with today to let them know I care? This may be my mom, a friend, a neighbor, or a colleague. I want everyone in my life to know they are valued whether we see each other often or not. Putting this into practice is difficult with jam-packed schedules and different lifestyles. It requires intentionality and prioritization.
- Work: What can I do today to help someone tomorrow? It's easy to get caught up in to-do lists and small action items, but most of those things don't matter much in the grand scheme of things. I want to scale at impact, so that may be making an important introduction, getting a client's project across the finish line, or teaching someone how to do something meaningful to them.
- Self: What can I do for myself today that allows me to feel good in the future? I have a long list of "why's" and "what's" that I still want to do, so maintaining my physical, mental, and emotional health is necessary to get through my list. It's great to know your purpose, but you can't activate it if you aren't taking care of yourself first.

What unique framework or service do you offer to your community or clients?

When I started WoosterMedia ten years ago, my vision was simple: to help people write and publish books. Whether through self-publishing, traditional book deals, or ghostwriting, my sole focus was delivering a published book. At the time, that was the entire scope of my business, and while it was fulfilling in some ways, it always felt like something was missing. My clients would spend months pouring their hearts and expertise into writing their books, but once they were published, they weren't sure what to do next.

The pattern was always the same. They'd post a few updates on social media, send out a handful of emails, and then sit back, wondering why the books weren't flying off the shelves. They didn't understand the bigger picture—a book is never meant to be a standalone offer. It's a tool for leverage, a door-opener to bigger opportunities.

This truth hit me like a brick wall back in 2017 when my book *Ignite Your Spark* was released by Simon & Schuster. Just before the launch, the marketing person assigned to my book quit, leaving me with zero support. I had no social media presence, no marketing or PR plan, and no clear idea of what I was doing. To add another layer of difficulty, I was recovering from major lung surgery at the time. Talk about trying to swim upstream without a paddle. But I wasn't about to give up. I turned to what I did know—sales—and decided to shift my focus to bulk book sales. Instead of chasing individual sales, I pitched my book to organizations, nonprofits, and schools. My breakthrough came when a planner for a large nonprofit called We Day purchased nearly 4,000 copies for two of their events. That single deal was a turning point, and since then, I've sold thousands more books using this strategy. Today, teaching bulk sales is one of the first things we show our clients because of its incredible potential.

But the real shift in my business happened when I realized that the book itself was just the beginning. A book has the power to create incredible leverage when used strategically. It can lead to bulk sales, speaking engagements, digital programs, high-ticket coaching clients, licensing deals, and even more products like workbooks or curriculum. The key is to think of your book as a cornerstone—something that unlocks doors and positions you for long-term success. For our clients, a book becomes the foundation for the next three to five years of their dream career.

At Mindset to Millions, the company I co-founded with Wendi Weiss, our mission is to help people package their expertise into books, courses, speeches, and programs that monetize their knowledge and passion. We work with our clients to create a "red thread"—a strategic plan that connects all their offers, services, and products into one cohesive business. Our unique methodology combines business strategy, brainstorming, and deep customization to meet our clients' specific goals. No one else does what we do and can replicate the passion and heart we bring to this work.

Our process begins with identifying three key elements:

1. Writing a book that people genuinely care about
2. Creating multiple revenue streams
3. Building an engaged audience who become raving fans of your unique superpowers

We believe everyone has expertise and life experience that make them unique in the marketplace. Our job is to empower people to share that genius with the world in a way that creates impact and income.

One of the cornerstones of our methodology is a personalized mapping session. During these sessions, we work with clients to outline their book and build a roadmap for how it fits into their overall business strategy. But it's more than just the book. It's about the entire ecosystem that stems from it. Our clients leave these sessions with a crystal-clear understanding of their ideal audience, messaging, and next steps.

Our approach comes from years of experience, hard lessons, and wins. Over the last decade, I've written nineteen best-selling books, worked with hundreds of clients, spoken on stages nationwide, co-founded a SaaS company, created college-accredited programs, and helped hundreds of people turn their expertise into thriving businesses. Through it all, I've learned that the real magic happens when you leverage what you've created. A book should open doors to opportunities, create income streams, and position you as a trusted authority in your field.

It's more than just the process or the strategy—it's the heart behind it. What makes Mindset to Millions different is our belief that everyone deserves to live a life that reflects their passion and purpose. That's why we don't offer cookie-cutter solutions. Each client gets a customized plan to match their expertise and vision for the future.

Ultimately, we don't just help people write books; we help them build legacies. Whether that means creating programs, scaling their businesses, or speaking on stage, our work empowers our clients to make an impact that extends far beyond the pages of a book. Everything we do is designed to help them step into their next big thing with clarity, confidence, and purpose.

So, what makes what we do unique? We provide tools and strategies, but we also deeply believe in the potential of the people we work with. We create more than books; we create transformation for both our clients and the people they serve. And that's the kind of work that never feels like "work" but a mission for impact.

How were you able to transform a setback into a setup for success?

A few years ago, I had a business partnership go bad. We had nothing in writing, so it took nine months to legally separate. I learned that business partnerships need to be taken as seriously as marriage. You are putting your trust in someone else to share your values and the same level of integrity. Not all friends or family members make good partners. And not everyone maintains the same level of enthusiasm for the business once you get started.

With this new understanding, I confidently entered into a partnership with Wendi. We did two years of test projects to see how we worked together. Our values and goals are aligned, and we maintain healthy communication. Instead of sweeping things under the rug, we practice radical candor with the understanding that a foundation of respect and love is always at the root. I am having the best time of my professional life right now at age fifty-two, with someone I personally and professionally trust. I couldn't ask for more than that.

What advice would you give to someone considering entrepreneurship?

Let go of perfectionism and procrastination, which are often one and the same. Many new entrepreneurs spend so much time absorbing information, coaching, and training without implementing any of it. I spent the first six years of my career trying to make everything look perfect, from my website to my programs and offers and setting up CRMs and processes for things I hadn't yet tested. It was wasted time that could have been better spent serving people.

The ideal process, which is not unique to me, is to create quickly, put it out into the market, test, and then iterate. Failing fast and often is what separates real entrepreneurs from the rest. It's about learning quickly so you don't waste a lot of time building something no one buys or wants. Here's what that can look like for creating a group coaching program:

1. Research your target audience and pick one of their biggest challenges.
2. Identify the result you want for your program.
3. Outline the steps for getting there.
4. Create a sales landing page with your offer.
5. Launch it as a beta to a small group (charge less money for it).
6. Ask your beta group to give you feedback every step of the way.
7. At the end of the program, make changes based on what you learned.
8. Build out your new version and launch to a larger audience.
9. Repeat steps 5-8 every single time.

What is the best professional tip or advice you have received?

The number one tip I would give anyone (myself included) is to invest in coaching often. We don't know what we don't know. Hiring someone who has already done what you want to do is the best cheat code to accelerate your personal and professional growth. Doing it yourself will never save you money or time in the long run. You think it will, but it won't.

I am continuously investing in my growth. Currently, I am working with a functional medical group to learn how to integrate preventative health and well-being measures into my life. It includes working with a nutritionist, medical doctor, and mental wellness specialist. The results have been incredible, and I am learning health hacks that I will use for the rest of my life.

Professionally, I am invested in a LinkedIn cohort group teaching me how to brand myself and our business better. I am learning marketing, branding, copywriting, networking, and sales. In addition, I am surrounded by a community of our target audience for partnering and working.

This is why Wendi and I launched our Unleash Academy in 2024. We wanted to build a community of amazing experts, leaders, and entrepreneurs to mastermind and grow together. Every week, we meet online to learn new entrepreneurial skills, while sharing our challenges within a safe space. It is the community that Wendi and I have always wanted but never found. We are blessed to be surrounded by so many incredible people.

How can people connect with you?

I can be found at patriciawooster.com and on LinkedIn @PatriciaWooster.

WHEN I STOPPED TRYING TO FIT INTO SOMEONE ELSE'S BLUEPRINT FOR SUCCESS, I FINALLY STEPPED INTO MY OWN.

Debbie Golden

CHAPTER 3

FAITH, HOPE, AND FREEDOM: THE ENTREPRENEURIAL JOURNEY TO AUTHENTIC SUCCESS BY DEBBIE GOLDEN

In the years 2023 and 2024, my insecurities were laid bare.

Every doubt I'd ever had, every fear I'd buried deep, came to the surface. I had entered the online space at a time when everyone seemed to be reselling digital marketing courses, promising wealth and freedom from behind their screens. I clicked, I scrolled, and I wondered—*could this really be the way out?* But let me take you back to where it all began.

In 2023, I hit an emotional wall in my Corporate America job. After years of climbing the corporate ladder, checking every box, and meeting every metric, I felt...empty. My youngest son had just three years left before college. My middle son had a year and a half. My oldest daughter had already flown the nest, building her own life. The clock was ticking. The harsh reality hit me:

If I stayed on this path for another decade, my life would look exactly the same as it had for the past ten years—meetings, spreadsheets, endless KPI discussions, and business trips that left me missing precious moments with my family.

Corporate America had taken so much from me—time, energy, presence. It wasn't just the events and games I missed; it was the times I was physically *there* but mentally *gone*. Exhausted. Distracted. Numb. I wanted more for these final years with my boys under my roof. I wanted to sit at the dinner table without my phone buzzing. I wanted to cheer from the sidelines without worrying about Monday's presentation. I wanted to *feel* these moments, not just witness them from behind tired eyes. Deep in my gut, I felt it—a nagging sensation that something big was coming. Change was on the horizon, and it was barreling toward me like a freight train.

It was August of 2023 when the spark reignited. For the second time in my life, I felt that entrepreneurial fire flicker inside me. It was a random Monday night. I was curled up on my couch, scrolling through social media with a glass of wine in hand. That's when I stumbled across a few women claiming they were making thousands of dollars a month—right from their phones, working just a few hours a day. I paused. *Could this be real? Could this be my way out?* Little did I know that click, that moment of curiosity, would lead me down a path of profound personal growth. The next year and a half would stretch me, challenge me, and ultimately transform me. It wasn't just about income; it was about rediscovering my divine purpose. This was more than a career change. It was a life change.

And this…this is where my story begins.

In August of 2023, I officially stepped into the world of online entrepreneurship and social media. I was fueled by excitement, curiosity, and—if I'm honest—a touch of desperation to make this work. But here's the truth: *I started with a lie.* The people I was following—the ones claiming they were effortlessly making $10,000 a month, working just one to two hours a day from their phones—were, at best, embellishing. At worst, they were flat-out misleading. And boom—every insecurity I'd ever felt came flooding in.

What am I doing wrong?

Why aren't my videos getting views?

Why isn't anyone buying from me?

Do people just not like me?

Those thoughts became a relentless spiral, pulling me deeper into self-doubt. Instead of stepping back to reassess, I pushed harder. I worked longer hours. I poured every ounce of my energy—physical, emotional, and spiritual—into trying to "succeed." And it broke me. I was exhausted. Drained. Completely burned out. This wasn't just a failed attempt at a new business—it felt like a failure of *me.* Every other business I'd built before had been successful. I had faced challenges, sure, but nothing that tore me down like this. How could I be failing at something that seemed so effortless for everyone else?

In the stillness of exhaustion, I turned to prayer and meditation. And in one quiet moment, a thought washed over me like a wave:

Why are you competing in a game everyone else is playing? You've never done that before, so why start now?

That single question shifted everything. I stopped chasing someone else's version of success and started building my own. I created my own products, crafted my own message, and leaned into my deeper purpose: helping midlife women who are navigating their next chapter. That pivot changed everything. I started showing up as *me*—authentic, purpose-driven, and unapologetically real. And wouldn't you know it? That's when things started to click. My Instagram reels began to take off. They didn't just get *some* views—they went viral. As I write this, I have over 65,000 followers and several reels that have racked up between 20 to 30 million views each. I started attracting women who genuinely connected with my story and my mission. This wasn't just a business transformation; it was a personal one.

When I stopped trying to fit into someone else's blueprint for success, I finally stepped into my own.

What I wish more people would talk about when starting an online business—and what I had to learn the hard way—is that it's personal development on steroids. Every insecurity, every whisper of self-doubt, every instance of imposter syndrome, every moment of negative self-talk—it all comes rushing to the surface, demanding your attention. It's like standing under a harsh spotlight with your fears staring you down, daring you to blink first. And if that's not enough, it also reveals another harsh truth: our deep craving for *instant gratification.* This is why so many people throw in the towel. Not because they lack the skills, creativity, or potential, but because they're not prepared to sit in the discomfort long enough to push through to the other side. It's raw. It's humbling. And it requires a level of self-awareness that most people aren't willing to face. I faced that mirror, and I hit a fork in the road.

Yes, I was highly visible on Instagram. But deep down, something felt...off. My soul was restless. There was a hollow feeling that success metrics couldn't fill. So I paused. I stepped back, silenced the noise, and waited. I call it *a knowing*—that sacred, still voice that told me to wait on God to reveal my next steps. And He did. It's funny how you can hear advice a thousand times from other people—*wait for clarity, trust the process, God will show you the way*—but until you actually walk through it, the words are just noise. They don't land until you've felt them in your bones. For me, they finally landed.

Looking back at my life, I realize I've always had a gift for *moving through.* Through heartbreak, through disappointment, through crushing grief—I kept going. I remember moments during my divorce, sitting at my desk, tears streaming down my face while I typed out emails to clients. They never knew. My kids never saw the cracks. I carried the weight quietly because I wanted them to feel safe, to feel protected, even when I was unraveling inside.

I believe God gave me a rare gift: the ability to see my fears, my doubts, my pain—and refuse to set up camp there. I didn't deny them, but I also didn't allow them to become my home. Only recently have I realized how rare this is. And even more recently, I've come to see that the way I walk others—my kids, my friends, my clients—through their own struggles isn't just something I do. It's something I'm *called* to do. It's natural for me, almost second nature, yet it's deeply transformative for those on the receiving end.

This is the wisdom the experts always talk about, the advice I'd heard a hundred times before but never really heard: *Find something you're good at, something that comes naturally to you but something that is absolutely life-changing for someone else.* And there it was—my purpose staring back at me. This wasn't just business anymore. This was a calling and a mission.

After speaking with thousands of women, I've realized there's an epidemic of negative thoughts, emotions, and fear. It's not limited to women in the online space—it's in my family and my friendships. Honestly, nearly every woman I know faces these struggles. It often shows up as:

- Getting stuck in negative thought loops.
- Overthinking.
  - » Ego and self-judgment: *I'm not good enough. Why isn't this working for me? No one likes me.*
- Choosing to be offended, angry, sad, or lonely.
- A need to be in control.

- Holding tightly to negative life circumstances.
- Fear of change and moving forward.

Reflecting on all of this, my heart feels heavy, knowing how many women are trapped in their own minds, battling these relentless cycles of negative thoughts. I think about the countless conversations I've had with close friends and family members—each one sharing how these thought patterns have seeped into every corner of their lives: their marriages, their relationships with their children, their careers, and most heartbreakingly, their ability to dream, grow, and move forward. Where you focus your energy is what flourishes. When your mind is consumed by fear, doubt, and negativity, those thoughts can solidify into *beliefs*—beliefs that act as walls, blocking any chance of meaningful progress. But when you shift your focus—when you intentionally choose gratitude, love, and abundance—that's what begins to grow and take root in your life. It all starts with gratitude, because gratitude and fear cannot coexist.

The purpose of my business has become crystal clear: to help women break free from the grip of negative thoughts and energy so they can confidently take their next healthy step, whatever that may look like for them. Who would have thought that a gift I've carried with me all along would become the foundation of my online business? Well, besides God anyway.

Today, my business is a reflection of my collective experiences—physically, emotionally, mentally, and financially. Every struggle, every setback, and every breakthrough has shaped the work I do now. The truth is, if I had succeeded right away — if I had started making $10,000 a month from day one—I never would have confronted my ego, faced my insecurities, or felt the need to pivot toward something with deeper meaning and purpose. Those early failures weren't roadblocks — they were *refinements*. They forced me to grow, to stretch, and to lean into a calling far bigger than myself.

Looking back, I'm grateful for every moment of struggle because it led me to this beautiful place — a place where I can serve, guide, and empower women who are walking their own journeys of transformation. It's not just a business. It's my *divine purpose*. And I feel incredibly blessed to be living it.

One of the most powerful questions I ask women who are starting something new is: "What place are you coming from?" At the core, there are only two starting points: You're either coming from a place of lack and scarcity or from a place of abundance, love, and overflow. This distinction matters, and it shapes everything that follows. Let's explore this deeper.

Starting something new — especially a business — from a place of lack or scarcity rarely leads to success. This energy often feels desperate, almost like silently screaming, *Please pick me! Please buy from me!* When you're operating from this mindset, it creates an invisible wall between you and your audience. A few common signs of starting from lack include:

- Launching a business purely out of financial desperation
- Hoping for a quick buck instead of building long-term value
- Selling products or services you don't truly believe in
- Focusing more on what you can gain rather than how you can serve others

This is exactly where I started my online business journey. I thought I could jump on social media, resell digital courses, and make quick, easy money. After all, I'd been successful in so many other areas of my life. Why would this be any different? But I was *so wrong*.

The hard truth about building an online business is this: Your audience can feel your energy. When you're offering the same thing as hundreds, if not thousands, of others, energy becomes the differentiator. And mine? It reeked of desperation and scarcity. My messaging, my content—it all carried that invisible *please buy from me* undertone. And guess what? My audience picked up on it. As a result, I struggled—both with making sales and gaining visibility on Instagram. It wasn't my effort or my skills holding me back; it was the energy I was leading with.

The secret sauce to building a thriving online business lies in showing up with an energy rooted in love, abundance, and overflow. It's an entirely different game when your foundation is built on this mindset. This kind of energy naturally attracts growth, wealth, and dream clients. It's magnetic. For most people operating from this space, it stems from discovering their *divine purpose*— whether it's sharing something they absolutely love or a story of something they've overcome. Their passion, joy, and authenticity burst through the screen, and you can feel it. When you're driven by a deep desire to serve and help others from a place of overflowing love, people notice. They're drawn to it because it's genuine, and in a world full of noise, *genuine* stands out.

This was the turning point for my business. Coming from a corporate background, I was used to checking boxes, meeting targets, and sometimes disconnecting from the true impact of my work. But in entrepreneurship, that doesn't fly. You can't fake passion. You can't fake care. You have to genuinely *love* your products, your message, and the people you're serving. When I fully leaned into this mindset, everything shifted. My Instagram reels started reaching 20-30 million views. This is the space where you attract, not repel. When your energy is aligned with your purpose, your audience can feel it—and that's when the magic happens.

What is the "why" behind what you do?

At the core of everything I do is a divine purpose given to me by God. This isn't merely a passion; it's a calling. I want to help women, but I also feel deeply obligated to give back with a heart overflowing with love and gratitude for the countless blessings God has given me. One of His greatest gifts is the ability to keep moving forward in every season of life, despite my emotions, despite the negative thoughts, and despite the fear. It's not that I don't experience self-doubt or get caught up in my emotions—I do. But I've always carried an unshakable faith that God (or the Universe) has my back and that everything is ultimately working *for* me, not *against* me, and that it's going to be okay.

This is the essence of faith and hope. Without faith and hope, moving forward feels impossible. But with them, even the darkest moments become steppingstones. I want to share this gift with other women—to help them break free from fear, self-doubt, and negativity so they can move forward with confidence. I want them to know that it's safe to hope, because God is always guiding them, always working behind the scenes for their highest good. And here's something every woman needs to hear:

God made only one of you.

You are *unique*, you are *special*, and there is no one else on this earth with your exact purpose, talents, and voice. My mission is to empower women to embrace their uniqueness, step boldly into their purpose, and build the business—and life—of their dreams. When you move from a place of faith and hope, everything becomes possible. Doors open, opportunities flow, and outcomes unfold in ways you couldn't have imagined. Because with faith at the center, the possibilities are infinite.

What is the best professional tip or advice you have received?

Forcing business success simply *doesn't work.* Hustling harder, grinding longer hours, and pushing endlessly aren't the answers. Hearing this felt like a gut punch to me as a proud GenX'er. It goes against everything I was taught growing up. I've been working hard since I was twelve years old, and honestly, hustle and hard work brought me long-term success—until now. So, why is it different this time? Because I asked for more. I asked for something bigger and more meaningful. To step into the purpose God had for me, I had to become a different version of myself. And let me tell you—it wasn't easy. I had to shake off years of ingrained programming, let go of my ego (a humbling and, at times, painful process), and surrender to a new way of being. The biggest shift? Moving from masculine energy (pushing, forcing, controlling) into feminine energy (attracting, receiving, allowing)—a topic I'll dive into deeper another time. This shift was about moving from *pushing* to *attracting.*

Now, let me be clear: I still work hard at my business. I have product offers, funnels, automation systems, social media strategies, and ad campaigns. The difference isn't in *what* I do; it's in *how* I do it.

The entire framework of my business is now built on magnetic attraction energy. When I was operating purely from masculine energy—pushing, forcing, striving—it created a subtle but powerful repelling force. Clients could feel it. But when I shifted into alignment, leading with gratitude, love, and confidence, clients started to feel pulled in, not pushed away. It's not about doing less; it's about showing up with the right energy. And that shift has changed *everything*.

What unique framework or service do you offer to your community or clients?

There are countless incredible people out there helping others start their online businesses. Each one brings their own unique systems, strategies, and approaches to achieving success. With so many coaches often sharing similar advice, it ultimately comes down to finding someone whose message truly resonates with you or directly addresses your specific challenge. What sets me apart is my deep commitment to helping women who feel stuck in the gap—trapped by fears, emotions, and limiting beliefs that block their faith and hope from guiding them forward. I don't just offer advice. I provide practical product solutions designed to bridge that gap. My customer journey framework through my product offerings is built with intention and clarity, and it looks like this:

1. Products designed to help women break free from negative thoughts, emotions, and fears, empowering them to move forward with confidence and clarity
2. Products that empower women to discover their purpose, clarify their "why," and transform it into a profitable business

3. A course that equips you with the skills to launch your online business and set up efficient system automation

4. Products that get women visible on Instagram (your offers are incredible, but if no one sees them, then no one can buy them)

These offers are deeply interconnected—one cannot thrive without the other. Your messaging carries your energy, which is rooted in your purpose, shaping your offers and flowing naturally into your social media content. Together, they form a seamless framework where each element supports the next, creating an effortless and harmonious flow.

How can people connect with you?

I can be reached on Instagram @debbie.digital.

LEARNING TO TELL OUR STORIES HELPS US MAKE SENSE OF WHERE WE'VE BEEN, WHERE WE ARE, AND WHERE WE WANT TO GO.

Derrick Hatch

CHAPTER 4

THE POWER OF STORYTELLING BY DERRICK HATCH

The art of storytelling isn't confined to classic novels or critically acclaimed films; it is a power birthed within us, waiting to be unleashed. Stories help us make sense of our experiences and find meaning. We tell ourselves and others multiple stories (or narratives) about who we are, why we're here, and where we want to go. The stories we tell and give ourselves to reveal what's important to us. This is my journey of discovering the entrepreneurial spirit through the power of storytelling.

The Call to Adventure

Many great stories (both in fiction and real life) begin with what Joseph Campbell refers to as the "call to adventure" (*The Hero With a Thousand Faces*, 1949). This is when a character is invited to step out from the known comforts of daily existence and into the unknown potential of who they could become. One example of this pattern is found in Stan Lee and Steve Ditko's beloved comic book character Peter Parker (*Amazing Fantasy #15*, 1962). This scrawny outsider from Queens receives his call to adventure when he's bitten by a radioactive spider that gives him newfound abilities. Like Peter, we may hesitate, doubting whether we are truly ready to embark on such a quest.

My origin story begins in the southern California suburb of Temecula. In first grade, my teacher offered me the lead role of Farmer Mac in the school play. I didn't want to take it; I wanted to be in the choir, just like everybody else. Who was I to take that role? In my eyes, there was nothing special about me. But my mom challenged that self-narrative, explaining that if my teacher chose me for the part, then she must see something in me. When I accepted that call and performed in the play as Farmer Mac, something within me came alive. Newfound passions emerged for speaking and performing through the art of storytelling. I got a taste for a new narrative, one where I had something unique to offer.

The Conflict-Catalyst

Once a character accepts the invitation to a new narrative, they face an inciting incident that pushes them into a world of new dangers and possibilities. This conflict becomes the catalyst for undergoing a transformation. This is the moment when Peter Parker, in a moment of selfishness, chooses not to stop a criminal, despite having the ability to do so. The conflict-catalyst often serves as the first test, a threshold to cross in the search for meaning.

My dad encouraged my love for stories by introducing me to great books, movies, and music. This inspired me to write poetry, join the school's videography club, and play music in various bands. As I joyfully carved out a unique identity for myself, another narrative began competing for my attention.

In high school, I often found myself getting bullied when I tried to be myself. I searched for someone who would love and accept me for who I was. But teenage hormones and bad breakups created a toxic cocktail that poisoned my soul with the bitter taste of betrayal and heartbreak. All the while, I found myself saying and doing things that didn't reflect who I wanted to be. These struggles led to me feeling misunderstood, depressed, self-conscious, anxious, and fearful to fully be "me," because I didn't know who the real "me" was. The narrative that dominated my life was "I have nothing meaningful to offer anyone. Why try being unique?"

On April 4th, 2008, I drove home from school with my brother in the car. At a red light, I made a right turn into the left lane, completely unaware of the car rushing down the road at forty-five miles per hour. Upon impact, I lost control of the car and swerved off the road, up a small bank where an oak tree plowed through the windshield inches away from our faces. Once my head cleared, I pondered and wondered: *Why am I still here?*

Perhaps God was giving me a chance to straighten out my narrative, to take a more active role in the story

I was living. Did I want to continue allowing competing narratives to fracture my identity? Or could the stories I loved provide me with a vision for the stories I wanted to live? Inspired by stories of Jesus' love for the outcast, along with his passion for teaching, the rhythms of my life altered; this was the "me" I wanted to be. God had me here for a reason, so I must have something meaningful to contribute.

The Turning Point

Characters often experience an event or series of events that aid them in their quest for meaning and purpose. These moments are often described as "turning points" because they represent a shift in the character's narrative. Peter Parker's turning point comes when he learns that Uncle Ben has been murdered by the very same criminal he failed to capture earlier that day. Turning points often reveal a change in direction that one must undergo if they are to be successful on their journey.

Throughout the rest of high school, I explored different things I could offer others; this included teaching drum lessons (my first business), writing articles in the school newspaper, and composing songs for my alternative rock band. During one of our shows, I felt compelled to share my story with the audience. I hesitated at first because I didn't think I had a story worth telling or that anyone would care to hear. But a couple of days later, a girl who attended the concert messaged us on Myspace, stating that she wanted to end her life, and she didn't know what to do. Moved with empathy, I assured this girl she didn't have to navigate this alone. We agreed to get her teacher involved, and eventually she got the counseling she needed. Sharing my story became a catalyst for authentic conversation that could lead to genuine change.

This experience inspired my friend Adam and me to start a club on our campus called Broken Barriers. Over the next year, nearly a hundred students came through our club, telling their stories of survival, abuse, depression, and suicide attempts. This became a place where the barriers that often divided us were broken, and we were seen as human beings navigating life together. Despite the difficult conversations and my own shortcomings, I developed skills as a coach through active listening. The telling and receiving of stories became a sacred act.

I started getting asked to do teaching and public speaking (including a commencement speech at my high school graduation). My speeches and sermons were a blend of narrative analysis (from stories in the Bible, novels, and popular films) with personal development. These talks inspired students at other schools to start their own Broken Barriers clubs. For the first time, I found myself the head of an entrepreneurial enterprise that exceeded my wildest expectations. I got a taste of a better story, and I wanted more!

I entrusted Broken Barriers to a new set of leaders so I could focus on my next entrepreneurial endeavor: co-founding a recovery program for teenagers at my church. For the next three years, I balanced my theological education with mentoring teenagers as they expressed their stories of traumatic hurts, destructive habits, and emerging hopes. As I gained clarity about who I was, I found myself communicating my stories more effectively. This gave me the confidence to help my fellow co-leaders share their stories through public speaking. Not only could I offer my story, but I could also empower others to share theirs.

The Awakening

When the turning point shifts a character's narrative in a new direction, they often gain a sense of clarity. This is their epiphany, their "aha" moment, their "awakening." When Peter Parker shows mercy to the criminal who murdered his uncle Ben, he does so because of his awakening: "With great power, there must also come great responsibility." Although he didn't think it was his responsibility to stop the criminal, he now saw that this power must be wielded for good. The awakening in a story serves as the key to internal transformation, helping the character move forward with greater clarity and purpose.

When I married my wife, Tori, I knew I had found a lifelong partner who loved me for who I was, but also challenged me to grow as a person. We embarked on our next chapter by moving to Florida. This new adventure brought me into a diverse array of contexts, from serving the wealthy in a luxury hotel restaurant on Palm Beach island, to teaching literacy and life skills to students in the inner city of West Palm Beach. But even when I was teaching various classes (music, performing arts, and the Bible), even when I was married to the love of my life, I couldn't shake the feeling that something was still missing.

This became evident when I was asked to share my story at an all-staff meeting. The way I previously told my story now seemed incomplete. I wasn't quite sure what story my life was telling. This led to me deconstructing my narrative, struggling to reassemble the scattered pieces of my puzzled life. During this time, one of my coworkers shared a dream she had of me. In the dream, I was taking puzzle pieces out of my mind and trying to sort them out, only for God to hold them up and say, "This is all mine!" Instead of trying to find the missing piece, this dream challenged me to take the pieces I already had and ask God what to do with them.

So much in my life was changing: I had become a father, purchased my first home, and been promoted to creative arts director. I was feeling settled, but my coworker's dream kept gnawing at me. I spent the next two years taking an inventory of my life, carefully reflecting on every piece of my identity.

By 2020, there was a growing need for spaces where people could converse authentically about their experiences, problems, hopes, and sense of purpose. In surveying my career this far, I noticed how influential narratives are in shaping one's identity, both externally (via books, films, the media, history, culture, religion, etc.) and internally (the personal narratives we tell ourselves based on our experiences). So I embarked on a quest toward better understanding the role of storytelling in personal development, reading books like Donald Miller's *A Million Miles in a Thousand Years*, Frank Roger Jr.'s *Finding God in the Graffiti*, and Jonathan Gottschall's *The Storytelling Animal*.

It was on this journey that I became acquainted with narrative therapy (also called narrative practice), a field of study that uses the language of story (i.e., the narrative metaphor) to help people make sense of their lives. The University of Melbourne and the Dulwich Centre accepted me into their master's program for Narrative Therapy and Community Work. For my thesis, I researched the implications of the narrative metaphor across various fields of study, including therapy, theology, the arts, and business. I developed these findings into a curriculum that could guide people in better understanding and telling their life stories using narrative therapy principles and practices. I then implemented that curriculum through a series of workshops for young adults and classes for youth. When both groups finished, they reflected on their experiences:

- "With guidance, I arrived at a knowledge of my own narrative like never before."
- "[This] took a lot of weight off me [because] I used to hold everything in, I don't really share with people; but I can be honest, I don't have to hide my feelings anymore."

- "I was able to feel safe in a room and share parts of my story that don't normally come up in everyday conversation. What I found was that as I was sharing, there was so much healing in simply being heard without any judgment or opinions given. There was space to be seen, and it was sweet."

What could I offer with this newfound research and practice? The connections between my passion for storytelling, my experiences in teaching, and my recent education in narrative therapy provided a revelatory clarity. Something was birthing within me.

The Leap of Faith

The awakening provides a character with greater clarity about how to enact their sense of purpose. Since success is not guaranteed, they trust that what they've learned will get them to the next step. This is their "leap of faith." After the death of Uncle Ben, Peter commits to using his powers responsibly through his alter ego, Spider-Man, which becomes the start of a new narrative. The leap of faith propels a character into the next chapter, thus repeating the cycle with a new call to adventure.

By the end of 2021, I was preparing to graduate as a masters-level narrative practitioner. Narrative practitioners find creative ways to restore people's agency by helping them reclaim expertise over their own lives. This occurs through an intentional process of challenging dominant narratives, while seeking to unearth and thicken alternative narratives that speak to who that person wants to become. My goal was to guide people through this re-authoring approach, but I wasn't sure what that was going to look like.

As I reflected on my journey, the pieces that made me who I am converged and offered a new way of seeing my story: entrepreneur. But at first, I didn't want to see this, because I was afraid to venture out on my own. Instead, I wanted to carry on as an employee, just like everybody else. Truthfully, I loved my job and didn't want to give up that guaranteed income, especially since I had a family to provide for. But my wife, Tori, encouraged me to think through other possibilities, assuring me that I have what it takes no matter what decision I made.

I came to see that my sense of purpose was oriented around somebody else's dream instead of my own. I wasn't satisfied living in a story where I missed out on my kids growing up due to long commutes and overtime hours, when by the time I got home, I was too burnt out to connect with them. My vision was to take a more active role in raising my daughters, Adeline and Autumn, but it required a more flexible lifestyle where I could organize my life around best serving them. Though I never set out to be an entrepreneur, I couldn't ignore the signs anymore:

- When I was too young to get a job at fourteen, I created my own source of income by becoming a private drum instructor.

- When I wanted to play music with friends, I started a band and learned about branding, marketing, and how to create something compelling that people can enjoy.
- When I started the Broken Barriers club on my high school campus and the teen recovery ministry at my church, I learned how to lead a team and implement an exit strategy.
- When I carved out unique positions for myself working at a luxury hotel on Palm Beach and a nonprofit in the inner city of West Palm Beach, I realized I didn't have to settle for the status quo.
- When I created that curriculum through my thesis project, I knew I had to create a vehicle to fully unleash my unique voice.

All of this inspired me to create All Things Narrative, a company dedicated to helping people tell their stories in ways that make them stronger, ways that inspire themselves and others to live a meaningful story.

The week of December 14, 2021 felt like the culmination of my story so far. My friends and I went to see *Spider-Man: No Way Home* in theaters, with a newer iteration of my favorite childhood icon learning "with great power comes great responsibility" as he gets ready to embark on his next chapter. Tori, the bridge between my origin story in California and my current chapter in Florida, threw me a combined graduation and thirtieth birthday party. I played drums with a band comprised of friends and family who spanned several different chapters in my life. Friends from church, coworkers from my nonprofit job, and even my friend Adam, who helped me start Broken Barriers, were all together. It was here that I officially announced All Things Narrative. The next day at church, I gave a sermon titled "Reflections on Turning Thirty," in which I spoke on the leap of faith, retelling my story in light of where I was going.

All things Narrative is my leap of faith, empowering me to create the lifestyle I've always dreamed of. I get to teach storytelling while coaching people how to communicate their stories impactfully through speaking, writing, and the arts. Using narrative practices, I help people navigate their challenges with greater intentionality and meaning. I also host events and podcasts alongside amazing friends and partners. Being an entrepreneur has allowed me the flexibility to be on staff part time at my church and work alongside nonprofits like the one I was employed at in the inner city. I even have time to teach drum lessons to the next generation of musicians. And most importantly, I spend more time with my family now (even welcoming my son, Benjamin, into the world as I write this chapter). Since I started All Things Narrative over three years ago, I am walking more fully in my purpose than ever before. I have become the unleashed entrepreneur!

"And once you live a good story, you get a taste for a kind of meaning in life, and you can't go back to being normal; you can't go back to meaningless scenes stitched together by the forgettable thread of wasted time." — Donald Miller, *A Million Miles in a Thousand Years*, 2009

What is the "why" behind what you do?

When life feels meaningless, we are often plunged into a meaning crisis, into a narrative that we feel lost in, and I believe that no one should feel lost in their own life story. Learning to tell our stories helps us make sense of where we've been, where we are, and where we want to go. Gaining this clarity empowers us to be intentional about the story we give ourselves. I believe that everyone has a story worth telling and worth living meaningfully.

What unique framework or service do you offer to your community or clients?

All Things Narrative offers a unique approach to personal and professional development. Our services include:

The Art of Storytelling: Our signature class offered to both adults and youth. Participants learn various forms of storytelling while exploring their life stories through creative writing, public speaking, and literary/ film analysis. This curriculum combines insights and practices inspired by writers like C.S. Lewis, professors like Joseph Campbell, psychologists like Viktor Frankl, narrative therapists like Michael White, and entrepreneurs like Donald Miller.

Coaching: Our personalized coaching serves anyone who aspires to tell their story through speaking and writing. Using narrative therapy skills, my process helps clients piece together their stories with clarity, teaching them tried-and-true methods of how to bring that story to life. This also includes creating five-minute and one-minute versions of their story. Additionally, I help them create an archive comprised of different kinds of stories they can tell based on their various contexts and audiences.

Workshops: Our workshops provide organizations with enriching experiences that include *Storytelling for Speakers & Leaders, Archetypes & Problem Solving in the Workplace,* and *Crafting Your Testimony.* These workshops are adaptable for various settings, like staff development days, community events, and retreats.

Events & Speaking: Our Storyteller's Sessions are quarterly open-mic events in Lake Worth, Florida, that allow attendees to tell a real-life story centered around a specific theme. Additionally, I do speaking engagements on topics that include the power of storytelling, stories and youth development, narrative therapy, and the biblical narrative.

Podcast: The *Live a Meaningful Story* project is a podcast that explores the connections between the stories we love and live. Featuring conversations with experts and storytelling enthusiasts like Nicholas Natale, Joseph Wilson, and Jason Lynn, this podcast is for anyone who wants to better understand the art of storytelling, and how it to connects to everyday life.

What is the best professional tip or advice you have received?

When I started All Things Narrative, I struggled getting sign-ups for workshops. The first time I did my

Storytelling 101 workshop, I didn't get a single sign-up, despite weeks of email promotions, Facebook ads, and in-person networking. Desperate, I announced in a networking meeting (the morning of the workshop) that I would slash the price by 50 percent. I felt relieved when three people signed up. That evening after the workshop, all three attendees mentioned that they signed up for my workshop because of how passionately I pitched it, not because I reduced the price. Two of them signed up for my six-week class. And the third one handed me cash at the original price of the workshop, telling me, "You're worth it. Don't undervalue who you are or what you do."

How can people connect with you?

I can be found at https://linktr.ee/allthingsnarrative and on Instagram @allthingsnarrative

EVERY CONVERSATION IS AN OPPORTUNITY TO LEARN, MENTOR, AND INSPIRE BUT ALSO TO SERVE AS A LIFELINE IN OUR INCREASINGLY DISCONNECTED WORLD.

Jason Hill

CHAPTER 5

THE KING CONNECTOR: MY JOURNEY IN PIONEERING TECH-DRIVEN RELATIONSHIPS FOR A BETTER TOMORROW BY JASON HILL

Section 1: Early Life: Roots of Resilience

Growing up in Port Washington, New York, I was immersed in an environment that valued ambition and resilience. From an early age, I absorbed lessons of hard work, determination, and grit from my family. My mother—my biggest fan—instilled in me a tenacity that has been the cornerstone of my journey. She grew up in Washington Heights, NYC, where being streetwise was not a choice but a necessity. I remember her sharing vivid stories of overcoming challenges on tough city streets, emphasizing the importance of standing up for oneself and never backing down. Her fierce spirit and unwavering support meant that whether I was on the soccer field or racing a sailboat, I always had her voice urging me to be bold and fearless in the face of adversity.

My father, affectionately known as Captain Hook, was the entrepreneur in our family. Owning a store at the South Street Seaport, he demonstrated what it meant to take risks, innovate, and believe in one's own vision. I spent countless weekends watching him work tirelessly, learning that every successful venture requires a mix of creativity and relentless effort. While he managed the business, my mother ensured that I never missed an opportunity—a soccer game, a sailing race, or a family gathering. Their complementary roles in our family created an environment where hard work and creative thinking were not just encouraged but expected. I learned early on that success isn't given—it is earned through perseverance, dedication, and the willingness to think outside the box.

Early Passions: Sports, Sailing, and Poker

Being the youngest of three siblings, I often found myself in a competitive race to keep up with my older brother and sister. I had to work twice as hard to carve out my own space in academics, sports, and even family game nights. Yes, the youngest often gets away with more mischief, and I certainly pushed boundaries and tested limits. However, every challenge and every friendly rivalry helped mold me into the persistent, determined individual I am today. These experiences taught me that setbacks are merely setups for a comeback—a lesson that would serve me well in later years.

Outside the classroom, my interests were as varied as they were intense. I discovered my passion in sports. I wasn't content with simply being part of a team; I wanted to lead, to excel, and to be the best. This drive led me to competitive sailing in dinghies throughout Long Island Sound. The water, with its unpredictable currents and shifting winds, became both a classroom and a battleground. I learned early on about the importance of teamwork, strategy, and maintaining composure under pressure. These lessons—about reading the environment, anticipating change, and adapting quickly—became metaphors for life itself:

No matter how choppy the seas might get, there is always a way to navigate through them if you have the right mindset.

College at the University of Delaware further expanded my horizons. It was here that I discovered the exhilarating world of poker, a game that taught me not only about risk but about strategy, timing, and the human psyche. I vividly recall the adrenaline rush of sitting at a table with over 1,200 players in a major tournament, where I eventually placed fourth. Poker was more than just a game; it was an education in itself. The skills I honed there—calculation, bluffing, and keeping a cool head under pressure—translated directly into my professional life. Even now, when my wife and I travel to destinations known for their vibrant cardrooms, I am reminded of those early lessons in strategy and resilience.

Love, Life, and Lessons Learned

Meeting my wife was another pivotal moment in my life. As my college sweetheart from Ohio, she brought warmth, kindness, and a sense of calm into my sometimes chaotic world. Over time, she has evolved into my most trusted advisor. Known affectionately as "The Print Shop" for her habit of sending handwritten cards to friends and family, she has taught me that the smallest gestures often have the most profound impact. Her unwavering support and gentle reminders to always go the extra mile have been a constant source of strength. She showed me that success isn't solely measured in dollars or accolades but in the depth of the relationships we cultivate and the lives we touch along the way.

Our relationship has been a balancing act of love and ambition. While I chased after my dreams, she was there to celebrate every victory and help me learn from every setback. The sacrifices we both made—long hours apart, missed family gatherings, and moments of self-doubt—have only deepened our bond. Her support and constant reminders to go the extra mile for others have become a guiding principle in both my personal and professional life.

The Foray into Entrepreneurship: Lessons from Financial Advising

After graduating from the University of Delaware, I entered the demanding world of financial advising, a field known for its grueling sixty- to eighty-hour workweeks and fierce competition in the New York City and suburban markets. In an industry where the success rate for those under thirty was less than 3 percent, every cold call, every meeting, and every connection mattered. The pressure was immense, yet it was during these formative years that I discovered the true power of human connection. My work was driven by commissions and fees, making every relationship a potential turning point in my career. I realized early on that success was more than selling a service—it was about building trust and fostering long-term relationships.

In an effort to distinguish myself in a crowded market, I began integrating technology into my practice. Rather than viewing technology as a mere tool, I saw it as a strategic advantage that could revolutionize the way I connected with clients. This innovative approach soon opened doors I had never imagined. At the age of twenty-seven, I was invited to speak before 500 financial advisors about leveraging technology to transform their practices. This invitation was a turning point that validated my vision and reinforced the idea that innovation could be a game-changer in even the most traditional industries. For three consecutive years, I was honored as the youngest finalist for "Practice of the Year," a recognition that deepened my understanding of how creativity and resilience could overcome even the toughest obstacles.

A New Chapter in South Florida

In 2017, with a passion for warm weather and a lifelong love for boating, I made the life-changing decision to relocate to South Florida. This move was more than just a change in scenery; it was a complete reinvention of my lifestyle and career. Since childhood, I had visited my grandmother in Deerfield Beach, Florida, and had always dreamt of calling it home. After marriage and the birth of our two children in New York City, the time had come for a fresh start.

Relocating my family to South Florida presented a myriad of challenges. My entire client base was concentrated in the Tri-State area, and half of my income was derived from those relationships. I had to rebuild my professional network from scratch in an unfamiliar environment. The financial risk was enormous, yet the potential for growth was equally significant. I plunged into this new chapter with determination, driven by the belief that my innovative ideas could transcend geographic boundaries and find fertile ground in a new market.

During this period of reinvention, I began experimenting with new digital strategies. I started building websites specifically to generate life insurance leads, tapping into the power of the Internet to reach a broader audience. At the same time, I launched *The Shrimp Tank* podcast—a project born out of a desire to connect with successful entrepreneurs and CEOs on a deeper level. What started as a simple tool for networking soon evolved into a vital learning platform, a crucible where ideas were refined and strategies were tested. Every interview on *The Shrimp Tank* was an opportunity to learn from some of the best minds in business. I absorbed lessons on leadership, innovation, and resilience, all of which would later inform the creation of a revolutionary new platform.

The Shrimp Tank: A Masterclass in Relationship Building

The Shrimp Tank quickly became synonymous with deep, authentic relationship building. I earned the nickname "The Shrimp Tank Guy" among South Florida business owners because of my ability to connect with and learn from entrepreneurs at every level. Over the years, I interviewed over 500 entrepreneurs, including CEOs from companies such as Celsius, Tint World, 4Ocean, BurgerFi, TRX, Bolay, Just Salad, ShipMonk, Stretch Zone, SA Company, and 4EverYoung. Each conversation was a masterclass in resilience and strategy, reinforcing the idea that genuine relationships are the true currency of success.

These interviews taught me that success is not solely about having a brilliant idea but nurturing meaningful relationships built on trust, empathy, and mutual support. I learned to listen intently and to ask the questions that truly mattered. Every guest shared a unique story—a blend of triumphs, setbacks, and hard-won wisdom—that deepened my understanding of what it takes to succeed in today's competitive world.

The Epiphany: The Birth of Owwll

While I was deeply involved in these endeavors, the world was undergoing its own transformation. During the COVID-19 pandemic, when isolation became the norm and people were desperate for genuine human connection, I witnessed firsthand the shortcomings of traditional networking methods. People were home, craving interaction, yet the available tools simply could not deliver the immediacy and authenticity that everyone yearned for. In the summer of 2020, inspired by this collective isolation and need, I sat down and put my idea on paper: a platform that would allow professionals to connect in real time through one-on-one audio calls. I envisioned a solution that would eliminate the friction of endless emails and scheduling delays—a tool that would foster genuine, spontaneous connections.

By January 1, 2021, I had moved from ideation to action and begun the development of what would eventually become Owwll. Every step of the process was driven by the desire to bridge the gap between people who needed to connect instantly and authentically. I poured my energy into refining the concept, coordinating with a dedicated development team and rigorously testing every feature to ensure that the platform could deliver on its promise of immediacy and value.

The Evolution of Owwll: A New Era of Networking

On June 7, 2022, after months of hard work and relentless determination, I officially launched Owwll. The platform quickly began to attract users from various professional backgrounds who were eager to bypass the traditional hurdles of networking and connect in a more genuine, real-time manner. The launch of Owwll marked not just the culmination of an idea born during one of the most challenging times in recent history but also the beginning of a new era in professional connectivity.

Building Owwll was a journey of constant iteration. In the early days, we faced numerous challenges: debugging code, integrating user feedback, and navigating the unpredictable landscape of start-up funding. However, every obstacle only solidified my belief that eliminating friction in networking could fundamentally change the way we build relationships. Today, as I watch Owwll grow and evolve, I am reminded of every moment of doubt and every sacrifice made along the way.

A Personal Battle: Overcoming Cancer and Redefining Purpose

Later in 2022, after the successful launch of Owwll, my personal journey took another unexpected turn. I was diagnosed with cancer—a challenge that, while deeply personal and difficult, was entirely separate from the motivation behind Owwll. As chronicled in a *Sun Sentinel* article, the diagnosis came as a stark reminder of life's fragility and the importance of cherishing every connection. Although I underwent rigorous treatments and faced emotional and physical hardships, I want to be clear: Cancer was not the reason I built Owwll. Rather, it was an additional challenge that reinforced my belief in the value of genuine human connection. Even as I navigated this difficult period, my commitment to building a platform that could transform networking remained unshaken, and the experience further deepened my appreciation for every moment of authentic interaction.

As a father, husband, podcast host, entrepreneur, and leader, I have come to understand that sharing the hard parts of life is cathartic but also essential for inspiring those around me—my children, my family, my audience, fellow entrepreneurs, and the entire Owwll community. I believe that our vulnerabilities remind us that we are all human, and through these challenges, we grow stronger together.

Life, I've learned, is designed to knock you down. It will knock you down time and time again, but what truly matters is not the number of times you fall but the number of times you get back up. Every setback is an opportunity to rise again, wiser and more resilient than before.

I am deeply grateful to my Owwll community for entrusting me with the role of a leader and for the unwavering encouragement I receive. This support drives me to keep pushing forward with the conviction that we can create a better, more connected world. I refuse to give up until we impact millions of lives by transforming the way people connect and communicate.

I've come to realize that many people are more interested in the result than in the process it takes to get there. They want to be part of the outcome without experiencing the trials and tribulations that shape it. Yet, it is in the process—the hard work, the setbacks, and the relentless pursuit of improvement—that we truly discover who is worthy of our trust and dedication. These moments of struggle reveal our character and define our journey.

I am especially grateful to the Owwll brand ambassadors who have been by my side since our beta testing days, steadfastly supporting me through every twist and turn of our journey. Their unwavering dedication and readiness to answer the call, even in the toughest moments, have been a constant source of strength when my tank runs on empty. I also want to thank my local team in South Florida, whose accountability and encouragement have been crucial in keeping me grounded and focused. If you're reading this, know that your belief in our mission has been the fuel driving us forward, and I can't thank you enough for being an essential part of our story.

Throughout our journey, I've been able to reach out and lean on these remarkable connections on a weekly basis—a lifeline during challenging times. In many businesses, these bonds often remain unseen and unspoken, overshadowed by the final results, yet they frequently make the difference between failure and success. I firmly believe that genuine human connection is the heart of every thriving enterprise, and this aspect is often missing from traditional success stories. After all, no one can do this on their own, and it's our collective support that propels us toward greatness.

The Sacrifices Behind the Success

Building Owwll was not without sacrifices. As I detailed in a heartfelt LinkedIn post, the journey to create a groundbreaking networking platform demanded everything I had—my time, energy, and sometimes even my personal well-being. There were countless nights of sleep sacrificed to code reviews and strategy sessions, missed family events, and moments when the weight of uncertainty threatened to overwhelm me. I recall times when I had to choose between a critical meeting with a potential partner and spending a rare evening with my family. Each choice was painful, but every sacrifice was a steppingstone toward realizing my vision.

These sacrifices were not made lightly. I knew that if I were to build something that could truly transform society, I had to give everything I had. The long hours were balanced by the knowledge that every call, every interview on *The Shrimp Tank*, and every sleepless night was an investment in a future where connections could be made effortlessly. In retrospect, each moment of hardship reinforced my commitment and served as a reminder that success is not just about personal gain— it's about creating opportunities for others.

Ongoing Innovation and the Future of Networking

Today, as Owwll continues to grow and expand, I remain at the forefront of an industry that is constantly evolving. Our mission is clear: to eliminate friction in professional connections and to foster a community where expertise, mentorship, and genuine conversation can flourish.

In 2024, *Innovate South Florida*—a 300-page publication spotlighting transformative people, companies, products, services, and initiatives—honored us by including our story. Produced with South Florida Tech Hub on the INNOVATE platform, this groundbreaking book united top innovators from local and international arenas, featuring some of America's most prestigious organizations and leading minds in business, research, and academia.

Now, in 2025, as Owwll continues to grow with AI, strategic partnerships, and innovative networking features, we remain at the forefront of an ever-evolving industry. This accolade celebrates the thriving innovation in our region and reinforces our commitment to eliminate friction in professional connections. We are dedicated to fostering a community where expertise, mentorship, and genuine conversation flourish, propelling us forward as we work to impact millions of lives through meaningful, real-time connections.

The Lessons Learned: Philosophy and Reflections

Over the past decades, there are several key lessons that have guided my journey:

1. **Relationships Are the Real Currency**

   Every connection, no matter how small, can have a profound impact. The success of *The Shrimp Tank* and Owwll is a testament to the idea that deep, authentic relationships create a ripple effect of opportunities.

2. **Execution Over Ideas**

   While many people have great ideas, the true difference lies in execution. The long hours, countless sacrifices, and relentless drive to bring an idea to life have taught me that action is what truly makes the difference.

3. **Failure Is a Prerequisite for Success**

   Every setback, whether in my financial advising days or during the early challenges of Owwll's development, has sharpened my resolve. Failure is not the end but rather a steppingstone toward greater achievements.

4. **Always Add Value First**

   The core principle behind both *The Shrimp Tank* and Owwll has always been to provide value without expecting immediate returns. Building trust and giving selflessly have been the cornerstones of my relationships and my success.

5. **Resilience in the Face of Adversity**
   My battle with cancer was one of the most testing periods of my life, yet it taught me the importance of cherishing every moment and fighting for what truly matters. Overcoming a life-threatening illness reinforced the belief that perseverance, coupled with a strong support network, can help surmount even the greatest challenges.

A Call to Connect

My story is not just about business—it's about the human spirit, resilience in the face of adversity, and the unwavering commitment to creating value for others. I remain grateful for every challenge, every loss, and every moment of triumph, because they have all contributed to the person I am today.

Final Reflections

In reflecting on my life—from the relentless energy of my youth in Port Washington, the rigorous demands of financial advising in NYC, to the transformative years in South Florida—the recurring theme is clear: Relationships matter. They are the lifeblood of every venture, the unseen force that propels us forward, and the true measure of success.

Looking back on this journey, I see a tapestry woven with experiences from my early competitive days, the lessons learned from financial advising, and the pivotal moments that led to the creation of *The Shrimp Tank* and Owwll. Each chapter of my life—marked by moments of innovation, sacrifice, and personal trials—has contributed to the vision I carry today. I remain convinced that every connection, every conversation, and every challenge holds the potential to spark transformation.

My journey, marked by both personal triumphs and formidable challenges like my battle with cancer, has shaped a philosophy that I now pass on to every person I meet. I encourage aspiring entrepreneurs to act with intention, to take risks, and to always prioritize genuine human connections over superficial accolades. In today's fast-paced world, where digital interactions can sometimes feel cold and transactional, I am committed to reminding everyone that authenticity and empathy are the keys to meaningful success.

I am proud to say that the lessons learned from every interview on *The Shrimp Tank*, every challenge faced during my career, and every moment of personal sacrifice have culminated in a vision that is bigger than any one individual. Owwll is the embodiment of that vision—a platform built on the foundation of real, unfiltered human connection, designed to empower professionals everywhere to break down barriers and share their expertise without delay.

What is the "why" behind what you do?

My "why" is rooted in the belief that every meaningful connection can change a life. I built Owwll to eliminate the barriers to authentic networking so that professionals can connect instantly in real time and truly support one another. Witnessing the isolation during the COVID-19 pandemic—with significant increases in depression, anxiety, suicide, and divorce—reinforced that, as humans, we fundamentally need connection to flourish. My journey, from the competitive hustle in New York to navigating personal challenges, has taught me that relationships are the true currency of success. Every conversation is an opportunity to learn, mentor, and inspire but also to serve as a lifeline in our increasingly disconnected world. Ultimately, my goal is to see Owwll used daily by hundreds of millions of people around the globe—mirroring the reach of other major social platforms—and even integrated into classrooms to help people master the fundamental skills of communication.

What unique framework or service do you offer to your community or clients?

Owwll is the first platform that allows professionals to connect via real-time, one-on-one audio calls, cutting through the delays of traditional networking. Unlike platforms that rely on static profiles and messaging, Owwll is designed for spontaneity and immediacy. This unique framework creates an ecosystem where mentorship, partnership, and real-time advice flow seamlessly—a true innovation in professional networking.

How were you able to transform a setback into a setup for success?

Every setback in my life—whether it was the competitive pressures of the financial industry or later personal challenges—served as a wake-up call. During the isolation of COVID-19, I saw firsthand how traditional methods were failing us and transformed that insight into a revolutionary networking platform. While my later cancer diagnosis was an incredibly challenging period, it reinforced my belief in the importance of every connection rather than serving as the catalyst for Owwll. I learned that obstacles are opportunities to innovate and grow.

What role do collaboration and community have in your business?

Collaboration and community are at the heart of everything I do. The success of *The Shrimp Tank* podcast was built on the deep, authentic relationships I forged with entrepreneurs and business leaders. Similarly, Owwll thrives on a community-driven model where every user is both a mentor and a learner. By fostering a culture of collaboration, we not only grow as professionals but also create a supportive network that can overcome any challenge.

What is the best professional tip or advice you have received?

One piece of advice that has stuck with me is Steve Jobs' famous quote: "Here's to the crazy ones. The misfits. The rebels. The troublemakers. The round pegs in the square holes. The ones who see things differently. They're not fond of rules. And they have no respect for the status quo. You can quote them, disagree with them, glorify or vilify them. About the only thing you can't do is ignore them. Because they change things. They push the human race forward. And while some may see them as the crazy ones, we see genius. Because the people who are crazy enough to think they can change the world are the ones who do." This quote has been a guiding force in my life. It reminds me that success is more than ideas or intentions — it is the bold actions we take every day. The willingness to think differently and act on those ideas has led to my greatest achievements. I've also learned that it's perfectly okay not to fit in; being different often invites criticism, but I've come to see that ignoring the noise and staying true to my vision is one of my greatest strengths. Embracing my uniqueness and persisting despite detractors have fueled my personal growth and driven real innovation.

How can people connect with you?

I can be found on the Owwll App weekly accepting one-to-one phone calls! Also, I am on all social **@TheJasonRHill.**

I WAS GIVING MY POWER
AWAY TO OUTSIDE HEALERS,
NEEDING TO BE FIXED
WHILE NEGLECTING THE
INNER WORK THAT WOULD
EVENTUALLY MOVE ME INTO
A PLACE OF ACCEPTANCE.

Suzy Jeppesen

CHAPTER 6

BEYOND HEALING: FINDING LOVE AND PURPOSE IN MY IMPERFECTIONS BY SUZY JEPPESEN

I never thought I'd become a disability advocate. I also never imagined I'd be in a disabled body and be comfortable with it. Socially anxious for most of my life, I hid in the shadows. Riddled with shame and self-loathing, I never wanted to stand out as different. I tried desperately to fit in, to be liked, to meet the expectations I thought others had of me. Despite my struggle with perfectionism and the disease to please, I learned to see the very disability that singled me out as a gift.

In 2011, at age thirty-nine, I was diagnosed with polymyositis—a rare, progressive, muscle-weakening disorder that increases the risk of falls due to muscle degeneration. Over the years, I experienced numerous fractures that accelerated the muscle loss, eroding the strength I once took for granted. Year after year, I watched fearfully as my mobility declined, threatening my independence.

I spent years in denial—long before and after the diagnosis. I didn't let anyone in on the scary changes happening in my body. When my rheumatologist discovered my muscle weakness during a routine exam, I was still clinging to the belief that, somehow, things would return to normal. Denial felt safer than the terrifying reality that I had no control over what was happening to me. So, like many of us do when faced with the unknown, I numbed myself. French food and wine, dressing up to feel seen, and hours of mindless distraction on my computer became my drugs of choice.

That denial lasted until 2019, when my body started to betray me publicly. At work, I tried to hide the muscle weakness. I avoided stairs, using the elevator whenever possible, and pushed myself out of my office chair only when no one was watching. One day, after a fire drill, Lexie, my colleague, saw me struggling to pull myself up the stairs using the handrails. It was the first time someone at work had witnessed my weakness, and I felt a wave of embarrassment wash over me. Despite our closeness, I couldn't bring myself to talk about it. I was trying to be perfect and saw my muscle weakness as a deficiency. From then on, Lexie would quietly join me on the elevator after lunch to spare me the embarrassment.

The stress of my job as a case manager for veterans, many of whom were dealing with PTSD, addiction, and chronic pain, only added to my anxiety. We're subtly conditioned by society to feel less worthy when we're no longer able to work or contribute as we once did. My veteran clients reflected this: Many carried resentment as they felt used up and tossed aside by the military when their bodies and spirits broke down.

As I watched my illness progress, I had no idea what would become of me. Deep down I felt terrified of losing my independence. I had frequent obsessive thoughts about becoming confined to a wheelchair, being a burden on my partner, and ultimately ending up alone. Ruminating on and managing my health distracted me from my caseload demands. I punished myself by working at my desk anxiously for many hours without breaks, my body stiff, tense, and barely breathing. Eventually I realized that being in a constant state of fight or flight would not support my body's repair process. So, I worked up the courage to share my struggle with my manager, Marlene. On performance reviews she'd often say I was low maintenance. This time my usual composure gave way to tears.

Marlene showed great compassion by reducing my caseload, but as a people pleaser, I felt guilty about burdening my colleagues and assumed I was letting them down. Despite the lighter workload, the stress of my uncertain future and the progression of the illness remained. The constant worry left me distracted and accident-prone. One day, while making tea, I forgot to tighten the lid on the kettle and dumped boiling water on my hand, causing a second-degree burn. That night, I lay in bed sleepless with my throbbing hand submerged in ice water.

It was a fall down my friend Alina's stairs that finally woke me up. I had visited her for a walk and dinner, though we couldn't walk because my foot was swollen and cut from two falls earlier in the week. Sitting outside on her deck, I looked down at my foot—red and angry around the open gash. There was no ankle, just swelling. My pretty, dark green pedicure stood out, as if trying to mask that I wasn't okay. After dinner, on the way back down from the bathroom, my leg gave out, and I tumbled down her stairs. Pain shot through me when I landed, inverted on my already injured foot, at the bottom of the staircase. This was my rock bottom.

As I stared helplessly at my feet, Alina, a nurse, urged me in a kind but firm voice to get medical support. I finally admitted I needed help. I reached out for an OT assessment, shopped for adaptive equipment, and made an appointment with a new doctor, Dr. M, to explore an off-label medication that had shown promise for autoimmune conditions.

For years, I had tried traditional medicine through my rheumatologist, but nothing seemed to make a difference. Since science and medicine don't know the cause or cure for polymyositis, the message I received was that my best option was to manage symptoms as the condition progressed. Yet the idea of passively watching my body decline filled me with terror. It triggered my deep fear of becoming a burden and ending up alone.

I turned to alternative health care, hoping it would get to the root of the problem. I jumped on the bandwagon of any treatment that showed promise: IV infusions, Rolfing, myofascial release, spinal network analysis, colonic irrigation, Chinese medicine, auricular medicine.

You name it, I tried it. I started each one with hope and ended up disappointed. I was giving my power away to outside healers, needing to be fixed while neglecting the inner work that would eventually move me into a place of acceptance.

Though I initially felt undeserving, I eventually decided to apply for disability so I could focus on my medical issues full time. When I broached the idea of applying for disability with Dr. M, she was challenging and abrasive. She had a strong bias against her patients going on disability, believing they'd waste their lives without purpose. She had no idea who I was, nor was she prepared to listen. The disability application process, which was already an administrative burden, became a grueling task without her support. Being the people pleaser I was, it took immense courage to speak up to an authority figure. I felt overwhelmed, but with emotional support, I rose to the challenge. While my experience with Dr. M was profoundly challenging, it pushed me to start advocating for myself in ways I hadn't before. But the deeper inner work hadn't yet begun.

Alongside all the other treatments, I attacked my illness from a psycho-spiritual approach. I saw energy healers, shamans, and channelers; dabbled in psychedelics to purge old patterns; committed to therapy, meditation, and 12-step programs.

Chronic illness is often stigmatized in spiritual circles, where I'd frequently hear that illness isn't real; it's just a result of your beliefs and focus. Being deeply spiritual, I bought into this, believing that if I raised my vibration, changed my mindset, and focused on the positive, I could cure myself. I'd been brainwashed by Law of Attraction teachings, and when I couldn't "fix" myself, I started feeling like a failure—a "bad" spiritual student. When I did gingerly share about my illness, I'd get hit with condescending Law of Attraction lectures or unsolicited advice about miracle diets and healing modalities. I know people thought they were being helpful, but it left me feeling isolated—like my experience was being judged or dismissed as a spiritual failure in need of fixing.

I had also internalized the societal judgment that it's not okay to be different. Our primal need to belong has us striving to look and sound like everyone else, creating shame and self-judgment around whatever makes us different. All the seeking I did for healing was rooted in not wanting to stand out as different or draw attention to myself. Women are meant to be able-bodied and attractive. No longer meeting that ideal took a toll on my self-esteem: I felt defective. In my building's underground garage, I'd wait in the car till the coast was clear. I didn't want anyone to see me struggling up the seven cement steps with my groceries—pulling on the handrails, pausing on each step to gather strength and lift my bags so I could climb without extra weight. On the way down, I'd usher others out of the elevator ahead of me so they wouldn't see me shuffling sideways down the stairs, my thighs too unsteady for a forward-facing descent. I held all of this with embarrassment and shame, thinking it made me less worthy, unattractive, old.

We often hear that "e-motion" is energy in motion, flowing through us in a healthy emotional system. However, as a child, I learned to suppress my feelings— especially anger—to keep those around me comfortable. I carried this habit into adulthood, trapping my emotions inside me. I sensed that my long-buried anger had become stuck in my body, settling in my legs and contributing to my muscle weakness. I turned to treatments focused on releasing this stored energy. Emotionally, I felt lighter, yet physically, my body remained unchanged. Frustration turned to anger—"Where is my healing, God?!"—and then to self-blame. "What am I doing wrong?"

The turning point came when I recognized a belief that had quietly sabotaged all my healing efforts: "I can't get better; no one can help me." How could I expect to heal when I didn't believe healing was possible? The spiritual community had taught me that to manifest something, I needed to believe in it, yet as polymyositis is rare and considered incurable, I hadn't found a single account of anyone in remission from it. I asked the Universe for faith that healing was possible.

Shortly after, I received an email from my myositis support group about Angelic Ingram—a woman who would later become a friend—who had gone into remission from dermatomyositis, a related illness. At the same time, I was reading *Dying to Be Me* by Anita Moorjani, detailing her recovery from terminal cancer after a near-death experience. For the first time, I felt a glimmer of possibility.

Within weeks of hearing Angelic's story, I found that my limiting belief had lost its grip. I began to trust that healing could happen if it was in God's plan. I surrendered the outcome of my illness, knowing I was never truly in control of it anyway. Instead, I focused on what I could control, taking responsibility for my experience of illness and disability.

I turned inward, deepening my relationship with my body and myself, committing fully to "the work." I began pausing throughout my day to tune into my experience whenever I noticed a shift in mood. I discovered how to re-parent my inner critic instead of blindly following it. I learned to feel my emotions rather than numbing them and built the capacity to do this outside of therapy. I started caring for my nervous system, calming and reassuring it during symptom flares or after falls instead of panicking. I spoke to my body with love and encouragement, celebrating small wins ("Look at you getting up all those stairs!") instead of criticizing it for perceived weaknesses ("You're so slow and weak; what's wrong with you?"). Trusting that my illness might be part of a divine plan, I stopped trying to "fix" myself and began loving and accepting my body as it is.

With newfound worthiness, I began advocating for my needs rather than viewing myself as a burden. I became "loud and proud"—speaking about my illness openly as a part of my life, not something to hide. Living this way, I found myself chipping away at societal stigma and inspiring others by example. I started focusing less on symptoms and more on what energized me, like being of service to others.

Through all of this inner and outer work, my attention shifted from seeing only the impediments of chronic illness and disability to noticing the gifts. Being visibly disabled forced me to stop hiding, to learn to ask for help, and to live more authentically. My body's weakness did not make me weak. In fact, it had given me strength I never knew I had.

Illness and disability have been my greatest teachers, for they've brought me to a place where I accept and love myself and my body as they are, *with* their struggles and imperfections. For years I'd been motivated to fix my "imperfections" to gain approval. This was one thing I couldn't fix. I wasn't broken, so "fixing" was never the solution anyway. Love and acceptance were.

One day I realized I no longer needed my illness to go away in order to be okay. I had found a way to live peacefully, to love myself and my body, and to live a life full of meaning. Sharing my story and impacting others give me a renewed sense of meaning and purpose—a purpose I'd lost when going on disability left me feeling less valuable, much like my former veteran clients did. I am no longer dependent on a health recovery to enjoy my life. I am grateful for the gifts this illness has given me: the ability to advocate for myself, a kinder relationship with my body, and much greater levels of self-acceptance.

My illness continues to progress, which gives me plenty of practice opportunities to work my new mindset.

Fortunately, the tools and mindset shifts I've cultivated on this journey are helping me to manage this with grace. As I write this I'm recovering from a hip fracture and using a walker. While the thought would have made me cringe a year ago, I am owning my walker without shame or self-consciousness. I notice the warmth and love that are radiated back at me when I am in full self-acceptance of my body's limitations and comfortably able to ask for and receive help.

Now I see that my journey has been about surrendering to the unknown, loving myself as I am, and discovering that true empowerment lies beyond the need for healing. I am finally enough as I am. Through this process, I've become not only an advocate for others but, most importantly, a compassionate ally to myself.

What is the "why" behind what you do?

My "why" is to empower people with chronic illness and disability to live fully without waiting on a health recovery. Through my work as a facilitator, speaker, and writer, I aim to share the mindset shifts that have transformed my own experience. By bringing light to the societal judgments and conditioning around disability, I hope to chip away at the stigma of illness and inspire others to step into their light.

I know the struggle of hiding what makes us different, feeling like we have to change or "get better" before we're worthy of being seen. My journey has been one of stepping out of the shadows and embracing what makes me unique. I share my story to help others find strength in their own differences, realizing they don't have to wait to belong or to contribute. They have something powerful to offer, just as they are.

What life lesson has created the most growth for you?

As a recovering perfectionist and people pleaser who was raised to not draw attention to herself, the gift of disability meant I could no longer hide or squash my needs. Where I'd been trying to fit in and do what others expected of me, my illness made me stand out. Suddenly I could be seen struggling with my mobility, and I needed to go off work, amplifying the risk of rejection. I had internalized societal judgments that it's not okay to be different, to be needy, to be idle. Having this illness forced me to challenge this conditioning and to love the things that formerly caused me shame.

What role do collaboration and community have in your work?

My participation with Healthy Love, an emotional relational education program and love lab, has been instrumental in my emotional recovery and ability to give back. It's given me a safe community to vulnerably share and process my experiences, to see and rewrite my story, and to embrace my shadow parts. It's been essential to my healing and the single most transformative thing I've done. I feel seen, felt, heard, and known in a way I never had before. Much of the work I'm now contributing was inspired by Healthy Love (https://www.Healthy.Love).

What unique framework or service do you offer to your community?

As a workshop facilitator, I empower individuals with chronic illness and disability to break free from societal conditioning, embrace self-love, and honor their bodies as they are. My goal is to help them recognize their inherent worth, even if they contribute differently than they once did. Through my workshops, I introduce seven empowering mindset shifts: cultivating Awareness of Thoughts & Stories; embracing The Importance of Feeling; deciding to Surrender & Trust; Soothing & Calming the Nervous System; actively Guiding the Body; Advocating for Your Needs; and finding Acceptance & Thriving. These shifts equip participants to cultivate resilience, self-compassion, and fulfillment, no matter their health circumstances.

What is the best advice you have received?

The best advice I've received is that everything is happening *for* you. This perspective has given me a curious, open mind. When I fractured my hip, my initial reaction was pure frustration. I was screaming in pain, thinking, *Not again! Why does this keep happening to me?* Yet by the time I was in the ER, I felt a shift and began wondering, *How could this be happening* for *me? What might I learn from it?*

One gift of this injury was the opportunity to release a major layer of perfectionism as I prepared to deliver a workshop on *Befriending Your Inner Critic*. My critical perfectionist was in full force, pushing me to over-prepare under the weight of my high expectations. During my recovery, living with my partner, Steven, allowed him to witness my stressed-out state. He gently supported me through the overwhelm and tears, helping me recognize the futility of my perfectionism. I decided to surrender to a new approach—trusting that I could show up authentically and allow the interaction to guide me.

This workshop became the first time I fully let go and allowed my Higher Power to work through me. That morning, I felt serene, free of my inner critic, and fully authentic with the participants. Letting go of control allowed the workshop to flow naturally, creating an incredibly moving and magical experience. Had I not fractured my hip, my rigid perfectionist would have shown up instead, delivering a far less effective workshop. Now I remind myself to stay curious during times of turmoil and trust that life is happening *for* me.

How can people connect with you?

I can be found at suzysunflower@icloud.com and on YouTube @suzysunflower.

CHANGING OUR MINDSET REQUIRES AN ONGOING COMMITMENT TO PERSONAL DEVELOPMENT AND OFTEN A FUNDAMENTAL SHIFT IN PERSPECTIVE.

e'Layne Kelley

CHAPTER 7

CRAFTING AN EMPOWERED MINDSET BY e'LAYNE KELLEY

*Y*ou can choose to let thoughts and stories about your past reside in your head, dictating your future, or you can choose to let them melt like snowflakes warmed by the sun.

I always believed I would die young. My father died at twenty-five, one month after I was born, and I never thought I would outlive him. This belief may have fueled my thirst for drugs and alcohol, because something drove me hard and fast toward an early death.

Around midnight, in the fall of 1975, I left a neighborhood bar in St. Petersburg after stopping to play a couple of games of pool and climbed into my green MG Midget. I hit third gear and headed down a familiar road. Suddenly, the double lines in the center of the road disappeared, and my car flew off a cliff and into the air.

I am going to die was my last thought before I lost consciousness.

When I woke up in the hospital, I knew it was a miracle I had survived. I learned that an enormous crater had been dug to construct the infrastructure where the interstate was being built. The four-lane road I'd traveled had an open-to-local traffic sign that loomed four feet long and eight feet high. It had led me to an unbarricaded, treacherous cliff.

This near-death experience sparked a profound spiritual awakening. There had been another "me" at the scene—a calm presence observing "me" driving off the cliff, with no fear or judgment. That "me" wasn't dying. That "me" had the same quality I had experienced in my youth: a spacious awareness, peacefully untethered from my everyday reality and thinking mind.

After I woke up, I wanted to find that kind of peace again. Being hurled off an interstate highway under construction and plummeting fifty feet seemed like a compelling reason to make some changes. Escaping death pushed me to confront my hollow lifestyle and evaluate my life's purpose.

While I experienced a profound shift in consciousness, my resurrection from an unhealthy and unfulfilling lifestyle didn't happen overnight. Armed with the experience of inhabiting a spacious awareness once again, I began stalking the elusive sense of peace I knew existed, determined to find its origin. I also knew my thoughts, beliefs, and behaviors constructed the barrier to dwelling in peace. My quest became to figure out how to remain buoyant under a barrage of negative self-talk and misguided beliefs.

My first mission was confronting my demons and gaining freedom from the chains of perfectionism, an unhealthy relationship with food, abandonment issues, poor self-esteem, and disconnect from my creative self. I was determined to no longer stew in my life of discontent and restlessness. Instead of letting life unfold without direction, I became an active participant, charting my life's course while simultaneously listening for a quiet voice within to guide me.

My path to entrepreneurship paralleled my inner work to retrieve and integrate the abandoned parts of my body, mind, and spirit. In my mid-twenties, as I attempted wholeheartedly to reconnect with the creativity that flowed effortlessly in my youth and early teens, an epiphany assured me flying solo in business was absolutely possible. The day I went to a Renaissance Faire in Sarasota, Florida, to get acquainted with my new Nikon camera changed everything.

After capturing images of elaborately dressed tightrope walkers and beautiful women on horseback adorned with flowing velvet- and lace-embroidered fabrics, I called it a day. Walking to my car, I encountered a man sitting beneath a grandaddy oak with a blanket spread in front of him. He was selling shell necklaces hand-painted with beach scenes for two dollars. I purchased one, and as the appropriately attired Renaissance man put the shell into my hand, a thought hit me like a lightning bolt. Whatever I make with my hands will always provide me with a prosperous livelihood. This knowing in my bones spoke louder than the constant voice in my head spouting self-effacing rants.

Seeing the world through a camera lens encouraged me to slow down and become more aware of my surroundings. As I meandered in nature, looking for interesting subject matter, I felt the breeze on my skin, smelled the newness of spring air, and heard the ospreys' high-pitched, whistling voices. My Nikon was inviting me to inhabit the present moment. The mind chatter faded as I focused on lighting, textures, and colors. Wearing the shell necklace that reminded me I could create a prosperous livelihood, I felt creative energy course through my body once again. It unleashed a ravenous appetite for sociology, psychology, art, and spirituality. My discontent and restlessness yielded to curiosity and wonder.

While finishing up the coursework for my BA in sociology, I made several sojourns to The Abode, the spiritual retreat center in Hudson Valley, New York. I began studying with its founder, Pir Vilayat Inayat Khan. My diet became meditation practice, which helped me cultivate an observant mind, and my thoughts continued to quiet. I worked in the garden, made new friends, and attended meditations and silent retreats. During one of my last stays at The Abode, I "heard" a message instructing me to leave my comfortable life in Florida and venture into the unknown.

I chose to listen.

After I left New York and returned to Florida, I put my belongings in storage, quit my job, found a home for my beloved cat, and left my adorable beach cottage, which had been my longtime home. I put my trust in something unknown and more significant than the familiarity of my restless discontent. With no money in the bank, no job waiting for me, and no Plan A, much less a Plan B, I hit the road with a sweet friend in his Volkswagen camper with fear and excitement in my belly. We zigzagged across America and parted ways in Walnut Creek, California.

Alone and jobless and with little more than the clothes on my back, I faced the blank canvas upon which I would paint my life. This time, inaction was not an option. I chose to craft a creative and spiritually aligned life using happiness as my compass. I landed a great job that paid for my master's work in transpersonal counseling psychology and Jungian dreamwork and saw a therapist weekly. Working with brilliant teachers at John F. Kennedy University awakened me to the dance between traditional psychological counseling, shamanism, and the connection between body, mind, and spirit. My bond with my teachers and fellow students was joyous and deeply healing.

I followed my open heart, which led me to a life's chapter on Maui and eventually back to Florida. My entrepreneurial life blossomed organically, fueled more by heart than strategy. Even when I worked in a traditional position, I opted for consultant roles to ensure autonomy. Over the decades, I co-owned four art galleries stocked with my creations, was Florida's Disaster Mental Health Coordinator, and was a national trainer assisting other states in setting up crisis counseling programs. For fifteen years, I managed a nine-acre art park. Currently, I love writing, making art, coaching, and teaching. Like many entrepreneurs, the businesses I birthed and the professions I managed were far-reaching, and at times many overlapped. Juggling several demanding businesses stretched my skillset, and I thrived on it.

When I started my first solo entrepreneurial business—making and selling hand-painted clothes with matching jewelry—I didn't take the time to research what specific tasks the business required to flourish. As a budding artist, I applied to and was accepted into several art shows. I bought a few racks to hang my clothes, a table, a tent, and two jewelry cases.

My first show was successful beyond my wildest imagination. My business took flight, but I had no idea how to manage or grow it, had hardly any inventory, and had a two-year-old son to raise. Trust me, this is no time to plan. I hadn't even asked myself soul-searching questions like whether the life of a traveling artist was what I wanted.

No matter your entrepreneurial endeavor, I suggest you ask yourself these questions I wish I had answered before starting many fledgling businesses:

- Do I feel passionate about building this business? Is it in alignment with my soul's desires?
- Do I have the temperament to make decisions promptly and manage the stress of owning my own business?

- Do I have the stamina and support to be an entrepreneur, or do I like the security of a regular paycheck and paid time off?
- What tasks need to be performed to make the business successful? Am I capable of performing them? Do I need to hire people or take classes to learn the necessary skills?
- Who owns a business like the one I want to launch and would be willing to share a snapshot of the day-to-day demands? When I visualize executing all the tasks, am I willing to put in the time it takes?
- How will I fund this business, and what are my financial goals? What support or skills do I need to handle my business's financial and legal obligations?
- What is my marketing plan? Can people in my network help me get the word out? Do I feel comfortable being in the spotlight to promote my business by doing podcasts, joining local business groups, recording videos, or being a public speaker? How do I want to grow my social media presence?
- What is my growth plan, and how do I measure success?

The answers to these questions will help you get a realistic idea of the commitment it takes to be an entrepreneur and determine if you have the personality to handle the unique challenges of going solo. When

I opened Out of the Way Café and Boutique, I loved designing the logo, painting the sign, designing the menu, and decorating and stocking the boutique. Even though I previously worked in restaurants, I had no desire to run a café at the time, and the bulk of the responsibility landed on my partner. That was a big problem since we hadn't budgeted for additional staff.

Over decades of being a serial entrepreneur, I've been ensnared in many challenges, and I'll share them so you can sidestep them. The challenges we encounter along the way often have similar themes. Unlike working for someone else, entrepreneurs must wear many hats to keep their business viable. Usually, we are not prepared or don't have the skills to perform the tasks the profession demands and are not financially solvent enough to hire trained staff. Another obstacle is that we might not know what tasks to delegate effectively, even if we have the necessary resources.

To avoid being overwhelmed with too many tasks or spiraling because of financial instability, put a date on your calendar to do big-picture planning at the beginning of a new endeavor and quarterly to make adjustments along your journey.

When you are on the entrepreneur track, how do you prioritize an avalanche of tasks and avoid being buried by the weight of responsibility overload? Putting fun and self-care time on your calendar is essential for work-life balance. Don't let work take precedence over your relationships, hobbies, or personal time. Learn to edit your life by releasing what weighs you down and embracing what lights you up.

For the last fifteen to thirty minutes of your workday, schedule the time to list the tasks you want to do the following day. By doing this, when you leave work, you won't mentally go over what you must do the next day while attempting to fall asleep. Also, before you finish your workday, use a project management tool like Trello and enter information and ideas you gathered that day to organize and access the information easily. This eliminates precious time lost on searching for phone numbers and meeting times.

My favorite way to stay focused and finish tasks promptly is to first group all similar functions together. For example, jot down separate lists: phone calls to make, supplies to order, subjects to research, and tasks to delegate. Put them in order of importance and timeliness. Tackle the most time-sensitive project first, set a timer for thirty minutes, and focus only on that one task. When the timer goes off, take a five- to ten-minute break and get a short workout or make a cup of tea. Rinse and repeat. This is the most rewarding organizational tool I use for time management. It's easy to execute, I remember to exercise and stay hydrated, and my productivity flourishes.

There was an obvious pattern to the ebb and flow of my serial entrepreneurial life. I was successful in every new business I created, but I'd get to a certain money threshold and wouldn't go any further. I knew my mindset was holding me back, maybe peppered with indecision about how full-out I wanted to play.

Then I had an epiphany. I realized there are two entrepreneurial pillars: tending to our business nuts and bolts and tending to our mindset. Most task-oriented hurdles we all encounter on the entrepreneur's journey are surmountable. With over thirty years of interacting with fellow entrepreneurs, I find our mindset is the most challenging obstacle to tackle. Recognizing and learning to work with our mental blocks is a lifelong practice in our personal and business lives.

Why are the task-oriented hurdles in our business manageable, while the mindset piece is much more difficult to traverse? Knowing the answer to this question will give you a new lens to observe and examine every aspect of your life. Drumroll, please…and the answer is that two different parts of the brain are used for each pillar: the conscious mind for the nuts-and-bolts pillar and the subconscious mind for the mindset pillar. So why does this matter? Let's find out.

When we are engaged in higher-level thinking, like designing and managing our businesses, we use the conscious part of the brain known as the prefrontal cortex. This area is responsible for cognitive functioning such as planning, decision-making, creativity, and focusing attention. It serves us in new skill development as we strategize and adapt to ever-evolving challenges in business. This part of the mind changes easily. Neuroscientists believe the conscious mind is engaged 5 percent of the time.

Our education system is based on learning by using tangible actions and strategies that can be methodically planned and executed. Projects like building a website, setting up a financial system, or creating a marketing campaign follow the formula we learned in school. In our business, we either learn the skills and logical steps to execute the project or pay someone to do it. The nuts-and-bolts pillar of business might overwhelm us with all its details and demands, but we know what we're dealing with since we have been raised to be strategic thinkers.

On the other hand, the mindset pillar is more challenging to navigate because it involves intangible elements such as beliefs, attitudes, and internal dialogues, which become wired in our subconscious mind from birth until age seven. Our thoughts and beliefs originate from what we've learned growing up. They comprise internalized voices from authority figures, parents, teachers, churches, social media, and institutions. Since we are young, we can't examine the validity of what we hear and assume that the statements of authority figures are true.

The subconscious mind functions as a cloud storage memory bank. It records all thoughts, emotions, and experiences, both positive and negative, and takes over when the conscious mind is occupied. It continually makes sense of information, searching its database to find repetitive actions that it turns into automatic movements.

The subconscious mind operates efficiently but not always accurately, as does the conscious mind. Since the subconscious mind can't reason, it doesn't judge, think, or change information easily. It doesn't understand time and space, so it records everything as if it's happening now. Subconscious brain activity operates habitually, ruled by instinct and learned responses—about 95 percent of the time—sorting information with lightning speed compared to the slowly operating conscious mind. This means our actions happen on autopilot 95 percent of the time.

Recently, I was on a call with thousands of people worldwide who were either working for themselves or desired to. The moderator asked the participants what stories or thoughts prevented them from growing a successful business. The chat sped by with responses from hundreds of people. The majority of answers were perfectionism, overcomplicating everything, imposter syndrome, fear of success, poor self-esteem, a perceived lack of interest in what one has to offer, fear of being too old, and fear of too many people doing it better.

Sadly, this is the information we feed our brains, the stories and thoughts about how we're not good enough, smart enough, worthy enough, or perfect enough. Since the subconscious mind can't reason, it tends to accept this information as truth, and every time we repeat negative things about ourselves, the beliefs are deeply embedded in our subconscious.

Some studies estimate that we think about 60,000 thoughts daily, and others say less. Of these thoughts, about 90 percent are the same thoughts from the previous day, and about 80 percent are negative. Thoughts are involuntary and occur automatically in the brain. Often, worry consumes our thoughts. The truth is that 85 percent of the things we worry about never happen. But what happens is we doubt our ability and are immobilized by fear, and our self-esteem is eroded. This is a significant disadvantage when we want to exit the corporate workplace and become the captain of our ship.

How do we shift our mindset so we're not operating on autopilot and stuck in a loop of self-defeating and self-sabotaging thoughts, beliefs, and actions? Changing our mindset requires an ongoing commitment to personal development and often a fundamental shift in perspective. We learn how to be the observer of our rote thoughts and behaviors. To emerge from a life running on autopilot based on subconscious programming, we must remain conscious of our desire to reprogram the brain and stay alert to where our attention is.

To reprogram limiting and negative subconscious beliefs, repetition is needed to rewire the brain's pathway. The subconscious mind understands the language of imagery and emotions. To rewire negative thought loops with affirming thoughts, take the negative statement "I am an imposter" and switch your statement to "I have wisdom to share with my clients." To deeply wire the new thought and belief, "see" yourself sharing wisdom with clients, "feel" how empowering it is to share your teachings, and "hear" yourself speaking to your client insightfully and enthusiastically.

Other ways to rewire your subconscious mind are to journal, replace negative thoughts with good thoughts, practice mindfulness to become aware of negative patterns, and repeat empowering mantras throughout the day.

Buddha said, "If you do what is good, keep repeating it and take pleasure in making it a habit. A good habit will cause nothing but joy."

What is the "why" behind what you do?

Little did I know that my personal journey to alleviate my suffering and get distance from punishing thoughts would become my "why," my life's mission. *I teach ageless women ready to alleviate their unnecessary suffering in order to release stress, detach from negative self-talk, deconstruct their barriers to happiness, and awaken their soul's purpose.* It's a rich inner journey, guaranteed to be a heart-centered, enlightening adventure.

What unique framework or service do you offer to your community or clients?

My framework and philosophy are outlined in my teaching memoir, Amazon #1 Best-selling book, *Roadmap to Ease, Release What Weighs You Down – Embrace What Lights You Up*. My book is brimming with shifts and exercises to assist you in letting go of obstructions blocking your freedom and happiness and recognizing the events that make you happy and empowered. By using this roadmap and following its nine trail markers and five shifts, you will quit wrestling with life as you learn to accept "what is." Trying to change what can't be changed will only create a life of stress and expectation.

Roadmap to Ease is full of questions to assist you on your awakening journey. If you feel struggle or resistance, choose one of these three questions to ground yourself and assess when you are returning to your inner self.

Ask yourself throughout the day:

- Am I moving in the direction of ego or divinity?
- Am I coming from a place of fear or love?
- Does what I'm focused on weigh me down or light me up?

Pay attention to your breathing as you observe your thoughts and behaviors, adjusting to move toward your divinity, coming from a place of love, and doing what lights you up.

You can work with me in several ways. I have a free private Facebook group, Gain the Wisdom Sisterhood Tribe, and I welcome you to join. I teach online and in-person classes and offer private coaching. Working together, I'll share wisdom, tools, and a roadmap to illuminate your soul's path, leading to happiness, ease, and awakening from unexamined thoughts and beliefs that cause unnecessary suffering. You will fully inhabit your authentic self and embrace life in the present moment.

What advice would you give to someone considering entrepreneurship?

We tend to focus on what we haven't accomplished and don't review the skills and life lessons we have achieved that make us who we are today. Go back to your childhood and think of the assignments or jobs you did where you felt proud of your accomplishment.

In the fourth grade, I did an assignment on folklore. I still remember feeling proud when I turned in my work, because I gave the project my all. That day, I went from a student who put in marginal effort on school projects to a person who went all out on her assignments. When I became a grant writer, I had the same feeling when I turned in a well-thought-out grant as when I handed in my folklore project.

In my early teens, one of my first jobs was assisting Mrs. Stambaugh at her laundromat. After I had worked there for a few months, she gave me a key and trusted me to open the store, collect the coins from the machines, and count the money. I remember how empowering it felt to be valued and trusted.

When people ask me how I directed large programs and trained and managed hundreds of people, I attribute my abilities to using the same skills I learned as a waitress. It required me to be graceful under pressure, problem-solve many situations at once, keep lots of details in my head, and be charming even when people were unreasonable.

Take a few minutes to review your life and reflect on the situations when you accomplished something or earned someone's trust and respect. How did it make you feel? When you have imposter syndrome or think you're not experienced enough to launch a new endeavor, remember everything you did, even as a young person, that made you the brilliant, capable, empowered person you are today.

What is the best professional tip or advice you have received?

If you try to build a new business or a growth mindset on your own, you're starting your new endeavor disadvantaged. Save yourself a lot of time and money by hiring a coach or finding a mentor who has taken the journey you're embarking on to show you the way. You will most likely reach your goals sooner.

How can people connect with you?

I can be found at eLayneKelley.com and on Instagram @elaynekelley_mindliberator.

HERE'S THE SECRET: SUCCESS DOESN'T COME FROM GRINDING HARDER; IT COMES FROM ALIGNING SMARTER.

CHAPTER 8

THE QUANTUM APPROACH: FROM AN OVERWORKED ENTREPRENEUR TO A QUANTUM PEAK PERFORMER BY MALVINA MESSLER

Million-Dollar Business

The champagne cork pops and everyone cheers! It's the year-end meeting, and the energy is electric.

"One million dollars in eighteen months!" my boss announces with pride. Then I hear the question, his eyes locked on me, "How did you do it?" The room gets quiet, everyone leaning in to hear my answer. I pause before I answer to reflect on the journey.

The truth is, I had taken a gamble when I accepted the role of VP of Business Development for Cloud Touch. The company had been stuck at $70,000 a year, scrambling to stay afloat—the team was exhausted from spinning their wheels with no results. But something about their potential struck a chord with me. I saw what they couldn't see yet: possibility.

And now, here we were, celebrating breaking the million-dollar mark. That's when I knew I had cracked the code to exponential success, unleashing potential into profit and going beyond what's predictable.

"Come on! What's your secret?!" they all insist. "How did you do it?"

I take a deep breath and respond: "I used the Quantum Approach."

If you're reading this and you've been wondering how to scale your success, break free from the grind, and unlock your own million-dollar potential—this is your sign. Because the same principles I used to grow that company are the ones I will share with you in this chapter.

Risky Move

When I returned home that day, something bothered me. While I was proud of what I had accomplished for Cloud Touch, there was a deeper longing in my heart. I had helped someone else achieve their dream—but what about mine?

The truth was that despite my executive title and six-figure income, I felt deeply unfulfilled. I kept this to myself because I didn't want to sound ungrateful. Deep down, however, I felt that I had more to offer; I knew I had been limiting myself—not playing full-out. I realized I had been settling for a life I had instead of creating a life I always dreamt of. It was time to rise, spread my wings, and unleash my full potential!

Success without fulfillment is the ultimate failure.
—Tony Robbins

That moment became the catalyst for my next bold but risky move: leaving the corporate world to create a business of my own. A business that didn't just generate money but made a real difference. I had a recipe for success, and I had to share it with others. That's how my coaching company, Life Unleashed with Malvina, was born.

Overcoming Fear

When I decided to leave my executive title and the comfort of a steady paycheck to bet on myself and build a business, my family and friends thought I was crazy. They were concerned that I was throwing away all the years I invested in building my corporate career. Some even said, "You're forty. You're too old to start over."

Self-doubt also started to creep in; a voice in my head whispered, "You've never done this before. What if you fail?" Another added, "If it took twenty years to build your corporate success, it'll surely take another twenty to succeed in business."

I could have given in to those limiting beliefs and allowed the fear to stop me in my tracks, but I was sick of living in fear. I was done playing it small and staying in my comfort zone. I wanted to be FREE. I wanted to become the CEO of my life—to live life on my terms.

That's when I heard the old Native American legend about two wolves that were fighting. As the tribe's chief was telling the story, his grandson asked which wolf would win, and the chief answered, "Whichever one you feed."

The same goes for the battle in our minds, the battle between our fears and our dreams. So I decided to starve my fears and feed my faith instead.

"Fear is a biological phenomenon, but it can be overcome with the power of your dreams."
—by Peter H. Diamandis, Steven Kotler

Redefining Success – No More Hustle

I had a big vision and an audacious goal of building a global coaching company. Before I could get started, I had to ask myself the following questions: "What does SUCCESS mean to me?" and "When will I know I have achieved it?"

I quickly realized that financial success was only a part of the equation. I was committed to building an impact business, the kind that would become a vehicle for me to fulfill my purpose, the kind that would give me freedom and flexibility and allow me to live my desired lifestyle. What SUCCESS meant to me was: FREEDOM, IMPACT, and FULFILLMENT.

"The New Rich are those who abandon the deferred-life plan and create luxury lifestyles in the present using the currency of the New Rich: time and mobility."
—The 4-Hour Workweek by Timothy Ferriss

Given that freedom was one of my core values, I didn't want to achieve success at the price of my health and well-being. I saw way too many entrepreneurs living in chronic stress, consumed by their work, with no time for family and friends, no time to take care of their health, not to mention time for hobbies and fun. This wasn't going to be me.

But how was I to make my bold vision a reality without the hustle? Could I actually have it all?

Can You Have It All? The Quantum Approach

It's time to dispel the myth that we can't have it all—that success must come with endless struggle, stress, and sacrificing our health and well-being. We've all heard the advice: "Work hard, and you'll be successful." This outdated belief is what keeps so many entrepreneurs stuck in a cycle of burnout. The truth is the hustle culture is an outdated business model that's quickly being replaced by the Quantum Approach.

The Quantum Approach stems from quantum physics and the concept of the quantum field—a vast sea of possibilities for anyone willing to see them. There is an infinite number of answers to our questions, an infinite number of solutions to our problems, an infinite number of ideas, opportunities, resources, clients, money, and even timelines.

> *"You are the observer of your own universe.*
> *Your observation collapses possibilities into reality."*
> **—Amit Goswami**

The Quantum Approach is the path to unleash our full potential and reach our goals faster and with more ease. But the Quantum Approach is not for everyone. It's for trailblazers who refuse to be confined by outdated, linear business models and old-school approaches. It's for bold thinkers who understand that the quickest wins come not from working harder but from thinking differently — because your business will never outperform your mindset.

Beyond Linear Thinking – Quantum Leaps

"The thinking that got us to where we are is not the thinking that will get us to where we want to be."
—Albert Einstein

I knew that if I wanted to fast-track my success, I had to do things differently. And it started with shifting my thinking. You see, the reason so many people cling to the idea that hard work is the ultimate key to success is because they've been taught to think linearly. Linear thinking follows a sequential path — going from A to B to C, one step at a time. The problem with linear thinking: It's slow, limiting, and keeps you stuck in a cycle of doing more to achieve more.

But there is another way. It's called Quantum Business Thinking. This is a style of exponential thinking that opens up possibilities by inviting creativity, collaboration, open mind, and flexibility. It's about stretching our imagination, focusing on the vision, and tapping into the quantum field of possibilities. That's exactly what I did.

I created a bold vision for my business, and I remained unattached to how it would be manifested. Once my mind was open to all the expected and unexpected ways I could reach my goals—even those beyond my imagination—my awareness grew. Suddenly, I noticed opportunities all around me—valuable resources, supportive people, and insightful ideas that could help me move the needle faster.

Let me give you an example. As I was building my coaching business, I could have done it in a traditional, linear way: offering coaching sessions to clients. But one day, guided by my intuition, I felt called to travel to Paris. Originally it was intended to be a solo trip, but as I remained open and not attached, two of my friends joined me, each with a deeply personal intention. For one, it was to celebrate life amid a cancer battle; for the other this was a reclamation trip after a difficult past. I created a meaningful itinerary that reignited our spirits, and we all returned home inspired and empowered.

That trip became the catalyst for my *She Rises in Paris Retreat*, which became my flagship program, launching me as an international retreat leader and global coach. Had I stuck to the grind and said "No" to what seemed like a lavish and unnecessary trip, I would have missed this quantum leap in my business.

The Pareto Rule and the Quantum Concept of Bending Time

"Doing less is the path of the productive."
—Timothy Ferriss

As I was reading *The 4-Hour Workweek*, a best-selling book in which Tim Ferriss redefines the traditional nine-to-five work paradigm, promoting the idea that time is not directly correlated to productivity, it reminded me of the quantum concept of "bending time" by focusing on high-value, high-leverage activities rather than the number of hours worked.

When we tap into the quantum field, we leap through time and achieve more with less. Tim Ferriss wasn't the first one to share insights on this matter. Long before him, Vilfredo Pareto, an Italian economist, discovered the 80/20 rule, now known as the Pareto principle. He observed that roughly 80 percent of outcomes are derived from only 20 percent of the inputs or efforts.

Following this rule when helping one of my clients with his business strategy, we recognized that 80 percent of his revenue was coming from a specific market: event planners. We decided to leverage it by allocating more marketing dollars and human resources to support this market. His revenue doubled within three months.

Embracing the quantum approach, I continued to challenge the idea that success must come from consistent, incremental effort over many years. Instead, I used quantum productivity principles such as the Pareto rule and began to leverage delegation, automation, AI, and outsourcing to achieve results much faster.

Quantum Alignment and Flow State

"FLOW is a state of consciousness where we feel our best and we perform our best."
—Mihaly Csikszentmihalyi

As I continued to build my business, I closely watched my competitors, replicating their strategies, but it quickly turned into a money pit. What worked for them didn't work for me. Even worse, I felt like I was losing my sense of self and blending in with the rest of the competition. I knew I needed to course-correct, so I stopped those activities that felt out of alignment with my core values and the way I wanted to build my business. Clarity began to emerge.

As I was building my service offering, I refocused on my passions, skills, and superpowers. I asked myself: What comes naturally to me? What lights me up? Then I turned my love for travel, my event-planning skills, and my knack for creating memorable experiences into luxury retreats in French castles and VIP days in California. I also combined my passion for fashion and my business skills to offer personal branding and styling services. Everything was rooted in my unique gifts and life lessons, like the deeply personal journey I shared in my book *Becoming You,* which became an Amazon bestseller.

This alignment with my zone of genius and my highest purpose allowed me to stay authentic, avoid comparison, and, most importantly, stand out from the competition. By remaining vigilant and releasing anything misaligned—whether it was habits, strategies, or clients—work became easier and more joyful! That's how I was able to tap into flow and at peak performance, bending time and fast-tracking my business growth further.

For too long, I've worn the struggle like a badge of honor, believing that "easy" equals "lazy," but it became clear to me that ease isn't the enemy—it is the reward for alignment, strategy, and flow. It's time we all find our passion and tap into flow!

Business Energetics – What's Your Frequency?

"Everything is energy. And that's all there is to it. Match the frequency of the reality you want, and you cannot help but get that reality. It can be no other way. This is not philosophy. This is physics."
—Albert Einstein

The biggest breakthroughs in my business came when I mastered my energy. You see, everything in the Universe, including us, boils down to energy, frequency, and vibrations. Our thoughts, words, and feelings have a certain energetic vibration and frequency. The lower the frequency, the more hardship we will experience. The higher the frequency, the more ease, peace, and joy.

Let me explain by sharing a quick story about one of my clients, Jenny, a dedicated real estate broker who, despite her hard work and relentless effort, wasn't generating any solid leads, and her pipeline was drying up. One day Jenny was invited to visit a friend in Europe—a once-in-a-lifetime opportunity. At first, she hesitated, feeling that the "responsible" thing to do would be to stay and double down on hard work. However, the desire to explore another European city and connect with her adventure spirit was stronger, so she gave herself permission to take the leap and embark on the trip. She immediately noticed something unusual. As she prepared for her trip—choosing her outfits, reading up on the history and attractions she was going to visit—she noticed an uptick in new leads and referrals. By the time she landed in Europe and began to enjoy her vacation, one of her listings had gone under contract. She returned home not only refreshed but also with a five-figure paycheck waiting for her.

When I asked Jenny to describe the emotions that accompanied her as she was planning the trip and then while traveling, she said she felt joy, curiosity, excitement, play, fun, bliss, and happiness—all *high vibration states of being*. She also felt more relaxed and more at ease. When I asked her to describe the emotions she felt prior to the trip, when her business was struggling, she recalled worry, anxiety, stress, sadness, and fear—*low vibration states of being*. Notice that her unexpected wins were not a result of what she was *doing* but who she was *being*.

Jenny's story illustrates how our frequency and vibration can impact our results in life and business.

Becoming Magnetic

I committed myself to mastering my energy and tuning my frequency to the frequency of what I wanted to attract to my life. It remains one of my most important practices to this day. And yet there was something else missing. I had premium offers but wasn't attracting premium clients. Moreover, I was spending way too much time attending networking events and trade shows, chasing leads. It was time to stop chasing and start attracting.

After doing a comprehensive audit of my brand, I realized that my messaging was all over the place, and my visual presence wasn't consistent across all platforms. It was costing me dearly. In today's fast-paced world, branding no longer revolves simply around logos and websites; it requires a quantum strategy that aligns your energy and messaging to attract the right opportunities, clients, and partnerships without the constant hustle. When your branding is magnetic, it's about more than appearance—it's about energy.

So I went back to the beginning. I did a brand makeover, starting with getting clear on my brand identity, brand essence, and brand personality. From there, I got clear on my ideal client, the language they use, and what inspires them. The final step was elevating my personal wardrobe and doing the brand photoshoot and professional video production to create visual assets that elevate my brand, convey my unique message, and resonate with the premium clients.

Once my branding was in alignment, I no longer needed to chase; instead, I created a powerful field of attraction that drew my ideal audience directly to me. During my next launch, I sold all my VIP packages within one weekend. This is the essence of magnetic branding: a shift from exhausting pursuit to attraction.

Upgrading Your Operating System – Making the Shift

"When you change the way you look at things, the things you look at change."
—Dr. Wayne Dyer

That's precisely what happened to me: I made a shift from an overworked entrepreneur to a quantum peak performer. I built a deeply satisfying business that gives me freedom to travel the world, speak on international stages, host luxury retreats in Paris and California, and spend more time with my family and friends, all while working on inspiring projects with my dream clients and making a positive impact helping other entrepreneurs achieve their dreams.

So here I am now, sharing my Quantum Approach with purpose-driven entrepreneurs who are ready to step off the hamster wheel and create exponential success—without sacrificing their health, happiness, or dreams. Because here's the secret: Success doesn't come from grinding harder; it comes from aligning smarter.

Are you ready to break free?

It's time to unleash your life.

OVERWORKED ENTREPRENEUR	SHIFT	QUANTUM ENTREPRENEUR
Success requires hard work and sacrifice.	→	Success flows from alignment and ease.
If I don't do it myself, it won't be done right.	→	I can create success through collaboration and trust.
I can't afford to slow down.	→	Rest is a strategic advantage.
I can't afford to be picky; I must say yes to every opportunity.	→	I only say yes to aligned opportunities.
My value is tied to how busy I am.	→	My value is tied to the impact I create.
I can't succeed without hustling 24/7.	→	I achieve more by doing less.
I have to choose between my business and personal life.	→	I can thrive in both business and life.
I have to take one step at a time.	→	I can leap into my next level now.
There is not enough time.	→	I bend time by operating in flow.

What is the "why" behind what you do?

I witnessed way too many purpose-driven entrepreneurs stuck on the hamster wheel, working harder and harder but not reaching their financial and impact goals. They needed to know there was another way. I made a commitment to helping entrepreneurs and visionaries break through the ceiling of their success and leave the rat race behind, unlocking purpose, impact, and authentic happiness.

What unique framework or service do you offer to your community or clients?

Motivated to provide a solution, I drew from my business experience, neuroscience insights, and quantum strategies to develop my Quantum Success Framework, a roadmap for leaders and entrepreneurs designed to help you unleash your genius and quantum leap your success! This cutting-edge system guides high achievers to harmonize ambition with authenticity and create quantum-level success without burnout. You can enjoy wealth, impact, and a dream lifestyle on your terms!

QUANTUM SUCCESS

- FREEDOM – Redefine success on your terms and live without compromise.
- WEALTH – Build financial abundance that supports your desired lifestyle.

- PURPOSE – Build a soul-aligned business and step into your life purpose.
- IMPACT – Unleash your potential and make the impact you were destined to.
- AUTHENTIC POWER – Release fear and lead with authentic confidence.
- HOLISTIC SUCCESS – Harmonize ambition, self-care, and fulfillment.
- BOLD LEGACY – Create a lasting legacy aligned with your vision and values.

Other Services:

- International Retreats (France, California, Thailand, Croatia, etc.)
- Public Speaking (Leadership, Mindset, Branding, Social Media, Self-Image, and more)
- Private and Group Coaching & VIP Days

How can people connect with you?

I can be found at malvinamessler.com and on LinkedIn @Malvina-Messler, and Instagram @MalvinaMessler.

IN THE END, IT'S NOT ABOUT BEING THE SMARTEST OR THE MOST TALENTED; IT'S ABOUT HAVING THE COURAGE TO FACE ADVERSITY HEAD-ON AND THE TENACITY TO KEEP GOING, WHEN OTHERS HAVE GIVEN UP.

Amber Stitt

CHAPTER 9

SCALE TO UNLEASH YOUR INNER ENTREPRENEURIAL SPIRIT BY AMBER STITT

For the past fifteen years, I have focused my professional life on helping medical professionals and business owners guard their most valuable asset—their ability to protect income. I believe that safeguarding and optimizing this resource is not only essential for financial security but also for creating the freedom to focus on purposeful, high-impact work. My hope is that the takeaways from this chapter motivate you to design a model that allows you to work more intentionally, reclaim valuable time, and unlock scalable revenue growth, creating a sustainable future. By doing so, you can unleash your inner entrepreneur.

Initially, I wrote this with the traditional business owner in mind—the kind with a storefront, a medical practice, or a virtual consulting business. Then I realized, not everyone aspires to that literal form of business. What I do know, however, is that everyone has the potential to achieve financial freedom through entrepreneurship—

in a way that's uniquely their own. You will often hear me speak about these "pathways" in life.

Today, I want to push you to think bigger—beyond what feels safe or comfortable. Imagine what it would take to unlock your full potential. This chapter isn't about chasing feel-good ideals like peace and happiness. It's about facing the hard truth: Real growth demands work, grit, and determination. It's about breaking through challenges, building a future that excites you, and stepping into the freedom you create for yourself through entrepreneurship.

When I was ten, my world was turned upside down. My two-year-old brother, full of life and potential, was tragically taken from us in an accident. The loss left a permanent mark on my heart; it also shaped what I would do professionally. In the aftermath, I watched my family cope with the emotional toll and struggle with the practical realities that come with such a sudden loss. This experience, though heartbreaking, gave me a deep sense of empathy and a clearer understanding of how people face life's toughest moments.

Maya Angelou once said, "You may encounter many defeats, but you must not be defeated." I took that wisdom to heart, using the pain of my own loss as a driving force to help others face life's uncertainties head-on. My mission became to help people plan in advance, offering the tools and resources needed to weather life's unexpected storms. However, my clients know that to make the change, they have to want to implement changes for themselves and for those they care about.

It is up to each individual to be the catalyst for change for any aspect of their lives. They have to choose to take action.

At its core, our insurance planning business is all about helping individuals achieve financial freedom by protecting their income first and integrating additional planning solutions. Our mission is to simplify what can feel like an overwhelming process, delivering expert advice and clear planning strategies. We break down essential steps to educate and provide efficient processes.

What also sets us apart is that we teach from experience—because we have participated in the processes ourselves. We've built our own financial freedom by applying the same principles we share with our clients. By equipping others with the knowledge and support that worked for us, we help turn their goals into real, lasting financial stability—empowering them to have a strong foundation during the good and bad times.

Goals within this chapter will help you tap into your mission and purpose so you can build the systems and surround yourself with the right people to stay on course. By leveraging your unique talents and network, you can create opportunities to generate new streams of revenue and other monumental moments. Even if you've never considered yourself an entrepreneur, I hope to spark the idea that you can be—because there are no set rules.

Whatever your story is—whether it's marked by tragedy or triumph—there's a moment in your life that connects you to the people you're meant to help.

By reflecting on those significant experiences and truly embracing them, you can extract the strength your history holds. This process not only grounds you but also brings clarity and confidence to defining your mission.

What life or business lessons have created the most growth for you?

My entrepreneurial journey kicked off during one of the most important moments of my life—the six months leading up to the birth of my first child, a little sister to my stepdaughter. Despite the opportunities provided by my immediate family's multiple businesses, I had a clear vision for a specific niche that deeply resonated with me. As my pregnancy progressed, I realized that starting my own company was the only way to truly fine-tune that niche and build the base necessary to embrace both motherhood and my passion for making a meaningful difference in people's lives on a schedule that worked for our family.

At first, I doubted my expertise when first going rogue and out on my own and often felt the urge to downplay my talents as a new business owner. I kept wondering, *Who will my clients even be?* I turned to a few friends in my business community for advice. Through those conversations, I learned the importance of trusting the pivot you feel called to make. With their support, I found the confidence to step into my potential and let my light shine.

We all have a unique calling and voice capable of making a positive impact. As I leaned into this truth, I began to clearly envision how I wanted to show up for my clients every day. I'm still building bridges to where I want to go, but having the choice to create that framework of my own started with taking the leap into entrepreneurship.

Your professional network is essential to your entrepreneurial journey. These people can help uncover talents you might not even realize you have and, in some cases, become your future business partners. Once you understand the drive behind what you do and give yourself some grace, your network often becomes a key source of support. They provide encouragement, keeping you grounded in your vision while offering fresh perspectives and highlighting strengths you may have overlooked. Their support can lay the groundwork that allows you to fully work to execute your goals to take meaningful steps forward and sometimes even find strategic partners along the way.

A great example of putting ideas into action happened about three years before my current business partner and I realized that a partnership between us could be mutually beneficial. We had attended several conferences at the same time, and while there, we would chat about business and have fun with other colleagues at dinners and breakout sessions. Six years later, not only have we built a successful partnership, but we've also worked together and independently on other strategic collaborations. It often starts with mastering your main focus, and once you're proficient, you'll find other opportunities to collaborate with others. Doing so is key to scaling your business and creating additional revenue streams—an essential step toward the financial freedom I've been talking about. It isn't just about the stock market or real estate but about other relationships and projects you can plug into but not have to show up to every day. Athletes and celebrities are great at this. They have their main thing, plus many other gigs they show up for during "off season" or in between projects.

Some of you may not have these inspiring people in your circle just yet. Maybe you are seeking a new, more supportive community. You can always look to successful leaders from the past to the present via books, podcasts, and more. No matter what age you may be, you can always start helping others through your passion for business at any time. We live in an era where we can learn from the successes of others, speeding up the learning curve by studying their journeys. There are countless resources available to help you develop a business mindset, create effective strategies, and grow your first business. Communication is the currency of life. Stay tuned for more on that soon!

What is the "why" behind what you do?

At the core of every successful business journey is a strong sense of purpose—a clear reason that keeps us going, even when things get tough. This baseline helps guide us through the challenges of building a business and provides the framework for our goals and dreams.

For me, it was shaped by the personal tragedy I mentioned earlier. After experiencing such loss, I saw up close the emotional and practical challenges my parents faced as a thirty-year-old couple during this time. This experience fueled my drive to take control of my own life—and to help others do the same.

Daily, I empower clients to plan for life's biggest challenges, providing them with the tools to be proactive through insurance planning and building a positive money mindset to navigate obstacles, stress, and grief. Unfortunately, life's challenges are inevitable, but I lead by example, sharing my story and personal experiences. My core principle within my planning is to take responsibility for myself so others don't have to take care of me.

Looking back on these events and the challenges within the financial sector in 2008 and most recently COVID in 2020, I've realized just how much unpreparedness can impact us—and it's something we still see today. Life will always throw challenges our way. I've seen firsthand how shock and stress can derail your work and mental clarity, pushing people into survival mode. I never want that for my spouse or daughters, and I don't want that for you either. Take the time to invest in yourself, your passions, and the people who support you. It's incredible how things begin to shift when you change your mindset. Opportunities will start to take shape. Stay consistent and truly want it.

I firmly advocate for "Taking Action Today" to initiate planning, recognizing that everyone has a different journey when it comes to setting financial goals and safeguarding their families. However, it is a must to do the work. I am determined to make a difference by helping others prepare effectively for life's uncertainties and encouraging them to take action while they are well and able to, and to introduce others in my alliance to help you get there. Dr. Amy Shah of Scottsdale says, "That no one is here to save you, you must save yourself." This quote resonates deeply with me, as I firmly believe it's up to each of us to take the first step and set the tone for our lives.

What is the best professional tip or advice you have received?

Back to business, there's one piece of advice that really resonated with me during one of my study groups, although it took me a while to execute it: "Hire early." At first, I was skeptical. Expanding the team felt premature, and I didn't want to add unnecessary overhead. Once I finally took the plunge, the results were immediate: My revenue grew approximately 70 percent. This decision didn't just boost my business; it changed the way I viewed leadership and growth. Once I trusted that hiring early was essential, that's when I saw the "x factor" in my annual production and revenue. With a team supporting me and my clients, things really started to take off. More hands on deck made all the difference.

Last year, I had the chance to see John Maxwell in person, and one quote of his really stuck with me: "Anyone can steer the ship, but it takes a leader to chart the course." I remember those early days when the idea of hiring felt overwhelming. The responsibility of managing a team and the fear of spiraling expenses made it all seem too risky. But at every conference and mentorship session, there was always this advice from peers: "Hire early, delegate, and know your billable rate." For years, I resisted this advice, convinced I could handle everything—being a business owner, spouse, new mom, and stepmom—all on my own. Little did I know, that mindset was actually holding me back. We were profitable and successful, but I had become the bottleneck that was keeping our company from doing more. Learning how to delegate felt amazing but took some time to get used to. My clients deserved more from me during our appointments.

This also requires a little humility. Please note that my husband is a core team member and partner and was encouraging me to make these changes. I had to trust the advice of others (spouses count too!) to evolve to help you achieve big goals. The internal work is a must, to be able to open your mind to possibilities. Often a coach can be a great bridge to the lines of communication. I don't think this work ever stops, so keep spending time on yourself and try to get your partners on board. This will be the guiding light when it isn't always fun, and it won't feel so lonely. Perfecting communication skills, as mentioned before, is key in work and at home with any relationship.

As I expanded my team, I realized the power of surrounding myself with individuals whose strengths complemented my own. It felt like unlocking a new level in a game. The energy and enthusiasm each team member brought to the table were contagious. This transformation was a wake-up call, changing not just my business but also my view on leadership. If you haven't invested in developing these skills, now is the time. Mastering these skills creates a continuous cycle of respect and positive interactions. And for those who never saw themselves as business owners, remember — we all need to grow and practice communication, no matter where we are in our journey.

Hiring early isn't just about delegation; it is about trust and empowerment. It is about building a foundation for sustainable growth. This decision was pivotal, setting us on a path where possibilities are endless, and each quarter we continue to innovate. If you're contemplating hiring, take this as your sign. Trust the process and watch your business flourish. This will move your business forward to where it needs to go. This decision is a game-changer, enabling you to work smarter, not harder, creating more time. It also helps you flex your leadership muscles, and all of us can use a little practice with that!

The benefits were immediate and substantial. Here's how hiring impacted our growth:

- Increased Efficiency: With specialized roles, tasks were completed more effectively, freeing up time for higher-level planning. I had more time for my clients.
- Enhanced Client Satisfaction: With more hands on deck, we could provide personalized attention, exceeding client expectations. The clients felt the team caring for them, and that extra touch elevated the experience.
- Scalable Operations: A robust team allowed us to take on more clients and projects without compromising quality. Having multiple team members to help carry the load meant more time for cross-training and less burnout.

Reflecting on this journey, I realize how important it is to trust in the process. Building a team is more than simply filling positions. It's creating a dynamic environment where everyone thrives. The synergy and creativity that emerged from our diverse team were key drivers in our success. This experience taught me that hiring isn't just an expense; it's a strategic investment in the future. By doing so, you create more time. More time to help clients can generate additional revenue while also creating more time for you to be present and true to your personal "why."

Implementing a Motivating Pay Structure

Another key part of scaling the team was having more incentives on pay. Incentives can be powerful motivators, and we wanted to harness that potential to energize my team. The idea was simple: Align the team's success with the company's success. Our most recent idea was by offering weekly pay incentives, which created a dynamic environment where everyone had a stake in the outcome that wasn't delayed weeks or months. This approach boosted morale and fostered a sense of ownership among the team. Around this time, I also incorporated weekly one-on-ones with my case managers who work with my clients directly. I made time to help them achieve their monthly goals, while helping to address some of the more complex client cases and questions. It also showed that I cared about their work and they weren't alone. P.S. It is fun to catch up too!

With the weekly meetings, my case managers could see that along with the financial rewards, it was recognizing effort and celebrating wins for all of us—clients too! Personalizing motivators to match individual goals and preferences made a significant difference. Some team members were motivated by bonuses, while others valued additional time off or professional development opportunities. By tailoring rewards, we were able to connect with each team member on a personal level, ensuring they felt valued and understood. Working on yourself and understanding what drives others is very important to a healthy and engaged team.

Productivity soared and our month-end data collection was exciting for all, and the quality of work improved as team members strived to achieve their targets. The production rewards created a friendly competition, encouraging everyone to push their limits. They were earning more and being part of a winning team. The positive energy was contagious, and it spilled over into client interactions, enhancing our reputation and client satisfaction.

Ultimately, the financial success we achieved was remarkable in a short amount of time, but the real victory was in building a team that was motivated, engaged, and passionate about their work. This experience taught me the value of investing in people and how aligning bonuses with business objectives can lead to extraordinary results. We can see this showing up as proof once a client finishes their steps for the year. We see their reviews online, and it is truly rewarding to know they are safe because of the planning we have done. They mention that they like having peace of mind with a team behind them too.

What advice would you give to someone considering entrepreneurship?

Starting a business isn't for the faint of heart. It takes persistence through challenges, and you must be relentless. This chapter offers you inspiration but an honest look into the life of a business owner. My best advice is to start with a deep dive on who YOU are so you can take your talents to the next level. This will help you on an individual level and will trickle down to other areas of your life. Your family and friends will see the shift. This requires an obsession with learning, growth, and aligning yourself with the right people (while sometimes feeling alone with your ideas). Not everyone will understand your goal until you start generating revenue. And be prepared that some never will. You must be deeply rooted in your purpose or mission. As mentioned before, surrounding yourself with other successful business owners is key to staying on course, especially since those closest to you might not be as supportive until the vision becomes profitable.

Success is not handed to anyone; it's earned through sheer grit and an unwavering commitment to outwork, outhustle, and outperform your competition. Scaling a business is no easy feat, but those who conquer are the ones who refuse to quit, no matter the challenges or setbacks that stand in their way.

Inside you is a strong drive and a deep desire to succeed. Tap into that fire, and let it unleash those ideas about wanting more, even if it isn't the typical career. Embrace the grind that it will take as each obstacle presents an opportunity. Stay true to your vision, and your team will respect the mission and want to succeed with you. Success is not a destination; it's a never-ending journey of growth, resilience, and unwavering determination, so know your personal reasons why. In the end, it's not about being the smartest or the most talented; it's about having the courage to face adversity head-on and the tenacity to keep going when others have given up.

As you embark on your first journey or continue evolving within your business, trust the creative process even if it isn't immediate, and watch your business flourish. Unleash your relentless drive and dream big, because many of those ideas are going to take shape for you if you let them. You and your clients deserve that. And don't forget to "take action" today!

How can people connect with you?

I can be found at StittStrategies.com and on LinkedIn @amberstitt.

TRUE PROSPERITY BEGINS WITH CREATING STABILITY WITHIN—A FOUNDATION FROM WHICH AUTHENTIC SUCCESS IN ALL AREAS CAN GROW.

Joey Torkelson

CHAPTER 10

BECOMING THE ENTREPRENEUR OF YOUR SOUL BY JOEY TORKELSON

M y career wasn't a climb; it was a gut-wrenching freefall into the murky, fizzing swamp of hospitality. Entrepreneurship? Maybe, although my main focus was raising three (soon to be four) beautiful children. Then came a dreary Monday in March circa 2001. Frank Sinatra was quietly playing in the background as I served dinner to the kids. The phone's shrill ring pierced the quiet, a metallic harbinger of doom. My father had collapsed behind the bar—his bar, the Waterfront Bar & Grill. It was his labor of love, his legacy, now forever marked by the tragedy of his sudden passing at just 58½ years old. That call ripped through the delicate balance of my life. The familiar greasy tang of stale beer turned suffocating, and the warm, inviting bar top suddenly felt cold, almost judgmental, as if it bore witness to the heartbreak that had unfolded.

He'd been my anchor all my life and my sole caregiver since seventh grade, a gruff yet loving presence who steadied or further jumbled my tumultuous teenage years?!? He was my world. And then, in an instant, he was gone—forever. Leaving me to inherit a legacy that in hindsight, I wasn't prepared for. His former sanctuary, once a vibrant testament to his spirited past, had transformed into a prison of inherited burdens and unyielding demands. The lessons I would learn from this were not just difficult or incredible; they were brutal and scarring, forged in the fires of grief and despair. That call changed my life and branded my soul!

The Waterfront's origin story commenced on September 5th, 1981, when Dad, aka Jim Scholle, and his lifelong friend and business partner, Joe Bell, purchased the Little Gallery Bar overlooking the shores of Delavan Lake. Rechristened the Waterfront Bar & Grill, it became my unexpected and unpaid apprenticeship. The air throbbed with the lingering aroma of spilled beer and stale cigarettes—a unique, albeit pungent, atmosphere. Its grand opening, September 13th, 1981, featured a meager thirteen barstools, plush red shag carpeting, and the world's largest urinal. The floor, however, sloped dramatically toward the jukebox and women's restroom, rendering even mundane tasks—song selection or restroom visits—surprisingly precarious balancing acts. After a cold shot of Jager, almost impossible.

The work on the weekends was far from glamorous for me at a mere thirteen. The laborious cleaning of countless beer mugs and shot glasses, each seemingly imbued with the lingering essence of a thousand regrettable choices. This concluded with the grim task of clearing cigarette debris from the neglected parking lot—a landscape more densely populated with discarded butts than a Hollywood gala. The upside of my newly found "chores" was in being able to choose the 45s that would be featured on the jukebox.

My sophomore year of high school offered a brief respite from the Waterfront's relentless demands, a fleeting month at A&W (remember the infamous widgets?), followed by a stint at Hardee's (conjure the iconic Moose Cups and Big Cookies), before I embarked on a four-year tenure at Eat n' Time, "Home of the Jumbo Burger"—yes, you read that correctly. There, the legendary Wally Plewe, a man who instilled in me an unwavering work ethic, reigned supreme. His mantra, "Time to lean, time to clean," was more than a motto; it was an ultimatum. Wally, who aggressively pursued my grandmother back in the day, insisted on the meticulous dusting of every single leaf on every plant, even during periods of minimal activity.

Subsequent forays into hospitality and golf club management with numerous, intermittent returns to higher education, punctuated by the transformative journey of raising my exceptional children, failed to diminish the persistent allure of the food service industry. I suppose some things, like the aroma of burgers and the hypnotic rhythm of a cash register, simply never relinquish their hold. I have referred to the food service industry as a drug of sorts; it's like an addiction. You either love it or have a love-hate relationship with it.

Dad and Joe decided to embark on a significant overhaul during the winter of 1992; they dramatically expanded the premises, incorporated an outdoor patio, updated the restrooms, and added twelve new barstools. A flat-top grill and deep fryer were installed, a somewhat dubious attempt to mitigate inebriation. The sensory onslaught—a heady cocktail of fryer oil, grilled hamburgers, and stale cigarette smoke—is one I'll never shake. I recall my outerwear spending more time airing out on the outside patio chair than in the closet, and I often found myself debating the merits of a 3 a.m. hair wash just to escape the Eau de "Old Bar." The struggle? Oh, it was real—and it reeked.

After inheriting the establishment, my initial focus was on keeping the beverages flowing and ensuring our regulars felt at home. While the work was far from glamorous, the financial rewards were substantial. However, as time passed, it became clear that Delavan had outgrown the quaint little bar. The original building, already over 100 years old when I took over, wore its age in every corner: brown paneling, tattered carpet, and walls permanently stained by decades of cigarette smoke. The nicotine literally dripped from the walls. Dad was far more interested in purchasing another Corvette than updating the tavern. Yet, one feature stood apart from the rest: our gargantuan urinal. Its size was legendary— so much so that, in theory, it could double as a shower for a small child. It was the kind of thing that left visitors baffled and amused, a quirky relic of a bygone era that seemed to capture the spirit of the place perfectly.

Frankly, the original Waterfront Bar & Grill was a venerable tavern, possessing enough rustic charm to be one step up from an "official dive bar" designation. Many of my friends shunned the place for obvious reasons; the lingering scent of tobacco clung to their clothes for hours. The aroma of a bygone saloon was far too pungent for the bleachers at their kids' sporting events. This aversion, ironically, fueled the Waterfront's transformation from a humble drinking hole into a respectable full-service restaurant.

On July 23, 2007, I laid the cornerstone of the new Waterfront *Pub & Eatery* in the parking lot next door. While the original Waterfront Bar & Grill is now a cherished memory, I meticulously built upon its foundation, creating an even more expansive space for celebration, adding the convenience of a drive-thru window and, most importantly, a from-scratch menu featuring upscale comfort food and an impressive selection of wine and craft beers. Although the space was transformed, my father's spirit remained an integral part of the Waterfront's soul and evolution. Little did I know that this venture would force me to confront my limitations and passions as I embarked on a profound self-discovery that tested the very limits of my resilience.

The first omen hit like a physical blow, a lion's roar in my gut. The next signs were much subtler, like quick, sharp needle pricks—small, but each one stung like a tiny, painful betrayal. Opening week arrived, a blood-red dawn. The Town of Delavan urged me to close due to sewer issues, confidently assuring me, "Your insurance will cover the losses," as the town clerk put it. That misinformation quickly unraveled, and I chose to keep the doors open. Twice, the town pressed its demands—a financial guillotine hovering, ready to cut tens of thousands from my already strained reserves. Each threat struck like a hammer, not just against my budget but against the fragile framework of my determination. Yet somehow, I survived—scraping, clawing, and pushing forward on nothing but defiant grit and a fiery, unapologetic "screw you" spirit.

Fast-forward to Mother's Day brunch, about five years in—a day that should have been my shining moment. Picture it: Chef #3 (soon to be ex-Chef), me, and what I envisioned as my Cinderella story—a champagne-soaked debut at the Entrepreneurial Ball. The Waterfront Pub transformed into a legendary feast fit for a queen, or, more accurately, for moms looking to brunch their way into bliss.

I arrived at the restaurant that morning riding the high of optimism that only comes with the busiest day in the restaurant world. I pulled into the front row, ready to conquer the day, only to be greeted by the ultimate omen: a dead black cat sprawled in the parking lot. Its lifeless eyes locked on mine, as if daring me to turn back. "No fucking way this is a good sign," I muttered, trying to convince myself that maybe a dead black cat canceled out bad luck. Spoiler: It doesn't.

Inside, chaos reigned. My new chef had prepared... absolutely nothing in advance? Buffet service? Apparently, he thought it was a suggestion, not a necessity. Guests were seated, and instead of a seamless brunch buffet, I watched in horror as he plated meals one painstaking dish at a time, like a slow-motion culinary train wreck. To top it off, we ran out of eggs — on Mother's Day brunch, of all days. Can you even imagine? No eggs at brunch. My only strategy? Champagne. I popped bottle after bottle, pouring glass after glass, hoping the bubbly would distract my guests from the unraveling chaos and the creeping sense of doom clinging to me like a bad perfume.

The stress of that day — and countless others — wasn't just physical exhaustion; it was a relentless undercurrent of anxiety that took root in my chest, mind, and even my dreams. Sleep became a distant memory as my thoughts were consumed by endless worries: the well-being of my kids, staff drama, and the terrifying uncertainty of my business's future. I still don't know how I didn't completely unravel under the weight of it all. On the brink of breaking down, I found myself retreating to the walk-in freezer to scream — a desperate attempt to release the pressure. No joke, one of my employees even stumbled upon me mid-breakdown once. My solution? Work harder, stay longer, and convince myself that sheer effort could outpace the chaos. But it was a losing battle, like pouring gasoline on a wildfire — every ounce of energy I gave only fueled the flames threatening to consume me entirely.

Every business struggle felt like a gut punch — a raw reminder of the deeper battles within. It's a crucible, shaping you into something stronger. The warning signs? I missed them, blind to the tremors before the quake. But success isn't about bracing for war—it's about strategy. Life is a chessboard where every move matters. One misstep can topple your kingdom, but a calculated, brilliant decision born from adversity can change the game entirely. The key is to recognize the power in those moments, claim it, and make your move with confidence.

Years later, I understood. The Waterfront, as a whole, was an albatross, a lead weight around my neck from the moment I inherited it, a suffocating legacy of my father's death. Its daily grind gnawed at my mind, sapped my very soul. The moment of release? Crystal clear. The eleventh hour of my divorce. During a discussion with my (soon-to-be ex) husband, my face wore a mask of weariness, and I blurted the words, "I'm going to sell the Waterfront to the first person who has cash." His response? "Sell it to me." "Done," I said. Two divorces for the price of one. Eighteen years together and a restaurant that had sucked the life from me, both gone. And only one lawyer bill. God bless the twisted, glorious, merciful irony of it all.

Fast-forward again, to 2025. I find myself thriving in a career that not only leverages my skills but also feels like the Universe's way of nudging me toward my true path. After heeding countless signs and messages that my previous journey was no longer aligned, I embraced a new direction into corporate America.

Today, I am a strategic beverage architect for a premier global flavor and ingredient company, spearheading an ambitious expansion across North America. In this role, I design innovative beverage programs for leading national restaurant chains, seamlessly balancing alcoholic and non-alcoholic options to appeal to diverse palates. Combining meticulous market research with advanced data analytics, I identify lucrative opportunities while optimizing profitability. I collaborate closely with sales and marketing teams, oversee impactful product launches, craft cutting-edge beverage concepts, design captivating promotional campaigns, and implement robust distribution strategies. Building strong, collaborative relationships with suppliers, distributors, and key stakeholders ensures flawless execution at every step. This career, though demanding, is incredibly fulfilling. It allows me to blend my competitive spirit, creative flair, and a lifelong love of food, drinks, and travel to drive remarkable growth for both my clients and the company I proudly represent.

Beyond my professional life, my passions deeply inform my work. I'm an avid explorer of the culinary and beverage world, dining out, discovering the best cocktail bars, and traveling the globe—only to find new iterations of what I love most. This ongoing quest for extraordinary dining and drinking experiences inspired me to start a blog, where I catalog my adventures and insights. This personal project fuels my creativity and keeps me connected to the ever-evolving world of hospitality.

Connecting the Dots

Life, much like business, is a venture filled with risks, rewards, and lessons. Both are intricately connected, teaching us how to navigate challenges, embrace growth, and define success on our terms. As entrepreneurs of the soul, our purpose is not merely to achieve outward milestones—a dream job, financial abundance, or even lasting love—but to cultivate the inner strength, balance, and wisdom that make those achievements meaningful.

Every career move and relationship is a lesson, revealing truths about ourselves and pointing us toward alignment with our higher purpose. Just as a business thrives on strategy, adaptation, and resource management, so, too, does life require boundaries, self-awareness, and mindful investment in our time, energy, and emotional well-being. A chaotic inner world cannot sustain meaningful work or love. True prosperity begins with creating stability within—a foundation from which authentic success in all areas can grow.

What is the "why" behind what you do?

I do what I do because I believe in the power of transformation—not just in business but in life. My journey has shown me that every challenge, every heartbreak, and every unexpected turn is an opportunity to grow, evolve, and align with your true purpose.

I've learned that resilience, adaptability, and embracing change are the keys to unlocking your fullest potential. Whether it's helping others create extraordinary dining and beverage experiences, guiding someone to launch a new venture, or simply inspiring people to take a leap of faith, my mission is to empower others to discover the entrepreneur within their soul and live a life of purpose, balance, and fulfillment. It's not just about creating success—it's about crafting a meaningful, joyful journey along the way.

When I chose to leave my past ventures and shift into corporate America, it was the Universe's way of showing me that my previous path no longer aligned. Signs, omens, and hard lessons led me to a career where I could apply both my creative and strategic talents while learning the value of balance. This shift wasn't merely professional. It was personal. It taught me that the same principles apply to relationships: They require intention, growth, and the courage to let go of what no longer serves us.

In love and business, the relationships we build are our greatest assets. Some offer incredible returns, enriching our lives; others drain our emotional reserves. Learning when to invest deeply and when to let go is essential. Not all connections are meant to last forever, and that's okay. Some people come into our lives to teach us, while others remain as steady companions. The key is to appreciate each encounter for what it is and to have the courage to move on when necessary.

Ultimately, both business and relationships are about growth, balance, and purpose. By approaching life as the most important enterprise we'll ever manage, we create a roadmap for fulfillment—not just in our careers or relationships but in the profound journey of becoming who we're truly meant to be.

What are your best professional tips and/or advice?

Owning a restaurant—or any business—is not for the faint of heart. It demands relentless hours, razor-thin margins, and a constant ability to pivot when challenges arise. The lessons I learned along the way weren't always pleasant, but they were essential to my growth as a business owner and leader.

1. Delegate, But Verify

Hiring a strong team is vital, but so is maintaining oversight. Trust is a powerful tool—until it's misplaced. Empower your staff to excel, but establish checks and balances to ensure the business runs as it should.

2. Address the Tough Conversations

Silence is costly. Avoiding uncomfortable discussions— whether with staff, partners, or even yourself—can lead to bigger problems. I learned this the hard way with a talented chef whose artistry in the kitchen didn't translate to profitability. Instead of having the necessary conversation about our financial goals, I avoided it, letting the issue fester until it was too late. Speaking your truth, even when it's uncomfortable, is nonnegotiable in business.

3. Strategic Rest Is a Business Decision

Taking time off isn't a luxury; it's a strategy. When a trusted friend advised me to close the restaurant one day a week during the winter, I hesitated but eventually took the leap. The result? Zero revenue loss and a much-needed mental reset. Sometimes the best business decision is one that prioritizes your well-being.

4. Don't Be Afraid to Seek Support

Running a business is a grind, especially in industries with slim profit margins. Restaurant food margins hover around five cents on the dollar, and even beverages—where the profit lives—come with deductions like credit card fees. Asking for advice and learning from others isn't a sign of weakness; it's a survival tactic.

5. Pay Yourself First

For too long, I treated my business as the sole beneficiary of my efforts, leaving myself out of the equation. That changed when I finally prioritized my own compensation. By paying myself first, I regained clarity, motivation, and balance—benefiting not just me but the business as a whole.

6. Friends Are Not Always Your Customers

One of the toughest lessons? Friends won't always support your business. Some will choose competitors, while others resist change altogether. When I replaced a thirty-plus-year dive bar with a new concept, a vocal minority boycotted the place out of spite. It's disappointing but inevitable. Business isn't personal, and understanding that is crucial to staying focused on what truly matters.

Each of these lessons came at a cost, but they shaped how I currently approach both business and relationships. Success requires adaptability, resilience, and the willingness to learn—about operations and about yourself. Success is not just measured by big, flashy achievements. I have come to realize that true success lies in the small, seemingly insignificant moments that make up our daily lives. For me, it's the simple joys like sharing a belly laugh with an old friend, taking a peaceful morning run on the beach, or having a heart-to-heart conversation with one of my children. These moments may seem small, but they hold great value and bring immense happiness.

Even after life's hardest moments—whether in business or in matters of the heart—we cannot allow fear to hold us hostage. Life is designed to challenge us, to break us open in ways that ultimately make space for growth. But those same challenges often leave scars, and it's tempting to retreat, to play it safe, to stop taking chances altogether. Been there. Done that.

After my most recent love interest ended—abruptly and painfully—I found myself slipping into hermit mode as I healed. It was as though I thought staying home, avoiding the world, would somehow shield me from further heartbreak. If I didn't put myself out there, I couldn't be hurt again, right? That was the logic anyway. But the truth is, that kind of self-imposed isolation is its own form of suffering.

During this time, I poured myself into work, convincing myself that overworking was a mode of healing—a way to distract from the pain and rebuild my sense of worth. But no matter how many hours I logged or tasks I completed, the ache remained. It wasn't until I began to focus inward that I realized I wasn't just running from heartbreak; I was avoiding the deeper, more complicated task of understanding myself.

Being the entrepreneur of your soul means embracing the inner work as fiercely as you tackle external challenges. It means peeling back the layers of hurt, disappointment, and fear, no matter how uncomfortable it might be. And I have tried everything—meditation, journaling, ketamine, DMT, and even ayahuasca, hoping for some epiphany to crack me wide open. Instead, the modalities only highlighted the steel shroud I had built around my heart—a shroud so thick it seemed impenetrable, even by the plant medicine meant to help me heal.

What I've learned is this: Healing is necessary but so is stepping back into the arena of life. Whether it's risking your heart again or launching a new venture after a business failure, taking chances is what keeps us alive and evolving. The lessons don't come from sitting safely on the sidelines; they come from showing up, messy and vulnerable, and daring to try again.

Life will always have its hard pills to swallow, but every time we take a leap—whether in love, business, or simply in opening ourselves to the world—we grow stronger. And the beauty of this journey is that every chance we take brings us closer to the person we're meant to become.

Building a life of purpose isn't limited to tech giants. It's a path open to all who yearn for a deeply satisfying existence. Truly successful individuals— those who thrive—are adaptable and courageous in the face of uncertainty, and they possess the wisdom to grow from setbacks. Discover the entrepreneur within yourself; nurture the spirit that drives you. Craft a life that resonates with your truest self. This could involve launching a venture, finding profound love, or simply waking each morning with a sense of joy and anticipation. Remember, serendipity often delivers the most breathtaking moments, and genuine triumph rarely adheres to a rigid script. Embrace the exhilarating peaks and the humbling valleys. Trust in the perfect unfolding of your journey.

How can people connect with you?

I can be found at LinkedIn @Joey Torkelson.
or on Instagram and TikTok: @drinksonjoey.

CONCLUSION

You made it.

By now, you've read the stories, the struggles, and the successes of entrepreneurs who dared to take a chance on themselves. You've seen firsthand what's possible when someone stops waiting for the "perfect moment" and starts building their dream, one step at a time.

The question now is: *What will you do with what you've learned?*

Because inspiration alone isn't enough; the world is full of people who have big ideas, who feel the pull toward something more significant, who dream of more freedom, impact, and fulfillment. But the ones who actually make it happen? They're the ones who *take action.*

Your Story Is Just Beginning

If there's one thing we hope this book has shown you, it's that success in entrepreneurship isn't about having everything figured out. It's about having the courage to start, the resilience to keep going, and the wisdom to adapt along the way.

Every entrepreneur you've read about started somewhere. Some with experience, some with none.

Some with resources, others with barely enough to get by. What they all had in common was the willingness to bet on themselves.

And now it's your turn.

What will your next step be?

Will you write that book you've been thinking about? Launch that course? Make your first offer? Step onto a stage and share your message?

Whatever it is, we challenge you to start **now**. Not when you feel "ready." Not when the timing is perfect (because it never will be). But now, while the fire is still burning inside you.

A Few Final Lessons to Carry With You

- **Clarity comes from action, not overthinking.** The best way to figure things out is to start. You'll learn more from doing than from waiting.
- **Your voice and expertise matter.** Someone out there needs what only you can offer. Don't let fear keep you from sharing your gifts.
- **Community is everything.** Surround yourself with like-minded people who will challenge, support, and push you forward. The journey is much easier when you're not doing it alone.
- **You are more capable than you think.** If nothing else, we hope this book has shown you that success is possible for you, no matter where you're starting from.

Go Build Your Legacy

The world doesn't need more people who play it safe. It requires more bold thinkers, leaders, and creators willing to take risks and do the work that matters.

And that includes you.

Whatever vision is in your heart, we believe in your ability to bring it to life. You've already taken the first step by choosing to learn. Now it's time to take the leap and make it real.

We can't wait to see what you create.

To your success and impact,

Wendi Blum Weiss & Patricia Wooster

ABOUT THE AUTHORS

WENDI BLUM WEISS

Wendi is the founder of The Speakers and Coaches Networking Society, an international audience of 18K+, where she provides education, resources, and support to help hundreds of purpose-driven entrepreneurs amplify their voices, reach more people, and elevate their impact.

A podcast host, published author of seven books, and an international speaker, she has spoken on college campuses, taught courses around the world, led international retreats, and hosted masterminds on topics that combine elevating your energy and harnessing your brilliance as it pertains to creativity, productivity, health optimization, and business success.

In 2022, Wendi joined forces with Patricia Wooster to empower entrepreneurs to stand out in a crowded marketplace by building their own audience, community, and brand through becoming best-selling authors, speaking on stages, and evolving their brand into a trusted authority.

Together, they bring the best of entrepreneurial wisdom, energy tools, and community to help more people unleash their greatness both personally and professionally.

PATRICIA WOOSTER

Patricia is the founder of WoosterMedia Publishing, where she helps experts, executives, and entrepreneurs codify their wisdom and leverage their expertise into books, digital courses, workshops, speeches, consulting, and media opportunities. Her clients include C-level executives, college professors, professional athletes, and media personalities who have landed agents, major publishing contracts, speaking opportunities, and bestseller status.

She is the author of nineteen books, including the award-winning and best-selling *Ignite Your Spark* with Simon & Schuster, and three entrepreneur co-author books with Wendi Blum Weiss. Her experience ranges from working with companies and organizations like Disney, Home Shopping Network, WeDay, Informix Software, Designing Genius, and KPMG to working with start-up entrepreneurs and influencers.

Today, she is partnered with Wendi Blum Weiss to teach entrepreneurs how to successfully brand themselves as best-selling authors, speakers, and experts in their field.

In addition to helping people unleash their superpowers, Patricia and Wendi are passionate about teaching entrepreneurs how to leverage their energy through functional health practices and the newest biohacking protocols to increase performance and creativity. They believe the key to a purpose-driven life is optimizing physical vitality and mindfulness, empowering entrepreneurs to establish themselves as influential thought leaders while prioritizing their well-being.

LEAVE A REVIEW

Before you go, if you enjoyed this book, will you please consider leaving a review on Amazon? As authors, there is nothing we appreciate more than reading reviews on Amazon and other bookseller websites from those who have enjoyed the book.

Thank you so much!
Wendi Blum Weiss & Patricia Wooster

www.ingramcontent.com/pod-product-compliance
Lightning Source LLC
Chambersburg PA
CBHW021150130626
46554CB00005B/1737